THE 100+ SERIES™

Reproducible Activities

Building Writing Skills

Laying the Foundation for Written Expression

Grades 4-5

By
Kelly Speer Hatfield

Inside Illustrations by
Tim Foley

Published by Instructional Fair • TS Denison
an imprint of

McGraw-Hill
Children's Publishing

About the Author

Kelly Speer Hatfield holds a bachelor's degree from the University of California at Riverside and a master's degree in education from the University of Houston. She has taught in Texas and currently teaches kindergarten through fifth grade as a writing specialist in Colorado. Kelly has written several books for the Instructional Fair brand, including *Building Writing Skills, Grades 2–3,* and *Genres of Literature.* She and her husband, Robert, also write poetry together.

Credits
Author: Kelly Speer Hatfield
Inside Illustrator: Tim Foley
Cover Illustration and Design:
      Matthew Van Zomeren
Project Director/Editor: Kathryn Wheeler
Editors: Diana Wallis, Mary Rose Hassinger
Graphic Layout: Tracy L. Wesorick

McGraw-Hill
Children's Publishing

*A Division of The **McGraw·Hill** Companies*

Published by Instructional Fair • TS Denison
An imprint of McGraw-Hill Children's Publishing
© 2002 McGraw-Hill Children's Publishing

Send all inquiries to:
McGraw-Hill Children's Publishing
3195 Wilson Drive NW
Grand Rapids, Michigan 49544

Building Writing Skills—grades 4–5
ISBN: 0-7424-0223-1

1 2 3 4 5 6 7 8 9 06 05 04 03 02

Table of Contents

Name _____

Terrific Towns

A **sentence** is a group of words that tells a complete thought. A **fragment** is not a complete thought.

sentences: Paris is in France.

I went to Tokyo many years ago.

Mexico City is very large.

fragments: Budapest, the capital of Hungary

in the beautiful city of Venice

Because Bombay is so old.

Write **sentence** on the line before each sentence. Write **fragment** on the line before each fragment.

1. _____ Tel Aviv is in Israel.

2. _____ The ancient cities of Sparta and Athens.

3. _____ St. Petersburg used to be called Leningrad.

4. _____ Cape Town is near the Cape of Good Hope.

5. _____ Because no one lives in the city of Machu Picchu.

6. _____ The town of Alice Springs lies in the middle of Australia.

Read the paragraph. Underline the fragments. Then, rewrite the fragments to make complete sentences. (Hint: Sometimes you can fix a fragment by making it part of another sentence.)

Pamplona is a city in northern Spain. A very old city. Every year, the city hosts a celebration. Bulls are set free to run through the city streets. People come from around the world to run through the streets with the bulls. Because running with the bulls can be dangerous. People are sometimes hurt.

7. _____

_____

8. _____

_____

You're the author! Write three fragments that describe a town. Make them into sentences.

        IF87135 *Building Writing Skills*

Name _____

Bothersome Brothers

A sentence that states something is called a **declarative** sentence. It ends with a period.

example: My brother never wants to take a bath.

A sentence that asks a question is called an **interrogative** sentence. It ends with a question mark.

example: How can you stand to touch that slimy lizard?

A sentence that shows strong emotion is called an **exclamatory** sentence. It ends with an exclamation point.

example: Oh, I can't believe you said that!

A sentence that gives an order or command is called an **imperative** sentence. It ends with a period or an exclamation point.

example: Give me my hairbrush.

All sentences are complete thoughts. They begin with a capital letter.

Rewrite each sentence with a capital letter at the start and the correct end mark. Use the color chart to color the picture.

1. leave me alone

   _____

2. brothers shouldn't bother their sisters

   _____

3. hey, I like my brother

   _____

4. what are you doing with that slingshot

   _____

5. my brother is nice

   _____

6. why do brothers yell so much

   _____

7. get out of my room

   _____

Type of Sentence	Color
declarative	purple
interrogative	red
exclamatory	blue
imperative	yellow

Name _____

Ant Facts

Every sentence has a **subject** and a **predicate**. The **subject** tells who or what the sentence is about. The **predicate** tells what the subject does, has, or is.

subject: <u>The leaf-cutter ant</u> grows plants for food.

predicate: The leaf-cutter ant <u>grows plants for food</u>.

Read each sentence. Circle the subject and underline the predicate.

1. Twenty thousand ant species live on our planet.

2. Some ant species can sting their prey.

3. Most ants live for less than six months.

4. Queen ants can live for several years.

5. Ant nests are often found underground or beneath logs.

Draw a line to match the subjects with the predicates that make the best complete sentences.

6. More ants   a. are a kind of insect that ants milk like cows.

7. The queen ant   b. travel in long lines like troops.

8. Army ants   c. harvests and stores grass seeds.

9. Aphids   d. live in the tropics than anywhere else.

10. The red harvester ant e. is the only ant that can lay eggs.

Write a predicate to go with this subject.

11. The ants at our picnic _____

_____

Write a subject to go with this predicate.

12. _____

_____ live in large groups called colonies.

Check it out! Read three sentences from any book. Identify the subjects and predicates.

Name _____

Mice and Men

A **compound subject** is made up of two subjects joined by the word **and**.

Sentences with the same predicate may be joined by using a compound subject.

example: Mice are a kind of mammal. Humans are a kind of mammal.

Mice and humans are kinds of mammals.

A **compound predicate** is made up of two predicates joined by the word **and**.

Sentences with the same subject may be joined by using a compound predicate.

example: Mice can climb well. Mice can run quickly.

Mice can climb well and run quickly.

Combine these sentences using a compound subject.

1. Humans can solve mazes. Mice can solve mazes.

    _____

2. Mice like to eat cheese. Humans like to eat cheese.

    _____

Combine these sentences using a compound predicate.

3. Humans are able to reason. Humans are able to speak.

    _____

4. Mice eat in their nests. Mice sleep in their nests.

    _____

Combine these sentences.

5. Humans care for their babies. Mice care for their babies.

    _____

    _____

6. Mice wake up at night. Mice look for food at night.

    _____

    _____

Name _____

Winter Olympics

Every sentence has a **subject** and a predicate. The subject of a sentence tells whom or what the sentence is about. A subject can be a noun or a pronoun. A noun is a person, place, thing, or idea. A pronoun takes the place of a noun.

nouns: medal, Sydney, competition, Carl Lewis, Bonnie Blair, games

pronouns: I, you, he, she, it, we, they

A complete subject includes the subject noun and all the words that modify or tell more about it.

example: **Athletes** challenge themselves at the Winter Olympics.

Circle the complete subject in these sentences.

1. One exciting event is the bobsled.

2. It is a sled race down an icy chute.

3. One of the most graceful winter events is figure skating.

4. The U. S. Women's Hockey Team won a gold medal in 1998.

Circle the noun or pronoun in the subject.

5. The athlete Bonnie Blair raced in the speed-skating event.

6. She won five gold medals between 1984 and 1994.

7. The 1998 Winter Games were held in Nagano, Japan.

8. Picabo Street won the super giant slalom in 1998.

Write your own pronouns for the subject in each sentence.

9. Alberto Tomba won two gold medals in 1988. _____ is a skier from Italy.

10. The Olympics begin with an opening ceremony. _____ is a time when all the athletes are together.

Write your own complete subject for this sentence.

11. _____ is my favorite Winter Olympic event.

Name _____

The Art of Sailing

The **-ed** and **-ing** endings are often added to verbs.

jump ⟶ jump**ed**   talk ⟶ talk**ing**

When you add these endings to some verbs, you have to change the spelling.
If the verb ends with a silent **e**, drop the **e** before adding the ending.

drive ⟶ driv**ing**   care ⟶ car**ed**

If the verb ends with one short vowel and a consonant, double the consonant
before adding the ending.

hop ⟶ hop**ped**   begin ⟶ begin**ning**

If the verb ends with a consonant and a **y**, change the **y** to an **i** before
adding the **-ed** ending.

try ⟶ tr**ied**   supply ⟶ suppl**ied**

If the verb ends with a consonant and a **y**, just add the **-ing** ending.

fly ⟶ fly**ing**   study ⟶ study**ing**

Rewrite these verbs with the **-ed** ending.

1. wish _____   3. hope _____

2. slip _____   4. cry _____

Rewrite these verbs with the **-ing** ending.

5. splash _____   7. wake _____

6. clap _____   8. reply _____

Write the correct forms of the verbs in the blanks.

9. Before computers and radar, _____ a boat across a sea was an art.
   a. to sail

Captains _____ their ships by the stars and with the winds. The ship's pilot
   b. to guide

_____ his knowledge of the sailing routes every day. The sailors on deck often
   c. to apply

_____ a sail to catch the perfect wind. If a good crew _____
   d. to trim   e. to work

together, they could guide a ship anywhere.

Time Travel

The verb **to be** is different from other verbs. These examples show how to make the subject and verb agree for the verb **to be** in the **present tense**. The present tense tells things that are happening now. First-, second-, or third-person subjects show who or what creates the action.

	singular (one)	plural (two or more)
first person—me	I **am**	we **are**
second person—you	you **are**	you **are**
third person—someone else	he, she, or it **is**	they **are**

Choose the correct present-tense form of **to be** to complete each sentence.

1. I _____ a very curious person.

2. My brother _____, too.

3. _____ you?

4. My parents _____ interested in time travel.

5. Together, my family and I _____ going to explore time.

The verb **to be** is different from other verbs. These examples show how to make the subject and verb agree for the verb **to be** in the **past tense**. The past tense tells things that have already happened.

	singular (one)	plural (two or more)
first person—me	I **was**	we **were**
second person—you	you **were**	you **were**
third person—someone else	he, she, or it **was**	they **were**

Choose the correct past-tense form of **to be** to complete each sentence.

6. I _____ lucky yesterday.

7. My parents _____ lucky, too, because deep in the woods, we found a time machine together.

8. We _____ walking in the forest when we met a strange man.

9. He _____ tall and thin and had long, golden hair.

10. He told us that he _____ the Timekeeper and that he had a time machine.

      IF87135 *Building Writing Skills*

Name _____

◆◆

Subjects and verbs must agree. This means the correct form of a verb must be used for the subject and the tense.

◆◆

Write the correct form of the verb to match the subject and the tense, past or present.

The Timekeeper invited us into his time machine. We _____**sat**_____ down and put on
(1. sit)

our seat belts. The cockpit was dark and musty.

"Where _____ you want to go?" he asked.
(2. do)

We all _____ at once. Dad wanted to see the start of the French Revolution in
(3. speak)
1789. Mom said that she _____ to see the Native Americans before the settlers
(4. wish)

came. I wanted to go ten years into the future.

"We _____ all the time in the world," the Timekeeper said, "but I have never
(5. have)

been to France. Let's go there." The time machine _____ and clicked. The lights
(6. hum)

blinked faster and faster. After just a few minutes, we _____ a bump. "We
(7. feel)

_____ here," said the strange man.
(8. be)

There _____ no windows, so we had to wait for the door to open. When we
(9. be)

_____ out, we stood in the middle of a cobblestone street. People _____ in
(10. step)   (11. run)

every direction. In the distance we _____ smoke and we _____ the sound
(12. see)   (13. hear)

of soldiers marching.

"What _____ going on?" I _____ a man dressed in rags. He answered
(14. be)   (15. ask)

in a language I _____ not understand.
(16. do)

The Timekeeper grabbed my arm and _____ me back into the time machine. As
(17. pull)

the door closed, we could see the rows of soldiers coming toward us. We _____ just
(18. leave)

in time!

11   IF87135 *Building Writing Skills*

Name _____

Ghost Towns

A **simple sentence** has a subject and a predicate and expresses a complete thought. Either the subject or the predicate may be compound.

<u>Aurora and Gold Point</u> <u>are ghost towns in Nevada.</u>

        subject   predicate

A **compound sentence** combines two simple sentences, or independent clauses, with a comma and a conjunction like **or**, **and**, or **but**.

<u>These towns</u> <u>used to be busy mining towns,</u> but <u>few people</u> <u>live there now.</u>

  subject   predicate   subject   predicate

Write **simple** or **compound** to show the type of sentence.

1. Ghost towns can be found all around the United States. _____

2. Some towns were just mining camps, but people still moved there. _____

3. Men moved to these towns for the adventure of finding gold. _____

4. The mines ran out, and the miners left the towns. _____

5. People still like to visit ghost towns today. _____

6. Some ghost towns are parks, and the states protect them. _____

Circle the letters of the two simple sentences in each group of three. Then, use a comma and the conjunction shown to rewrite the two simple sentences as one compound sentence.

7. (and)   a. A few men found gold.

              b. While they were digging in the hills.

              c. Other men came to find gold.

_____

8. (but)   a. The men still wanted to be rich.

              b. Gold is what brought the men to the towns.

              c. The gold soon ran out.

_____

Check it out! Research a ghost town in the western United States. What is the name of the town? Why was the town established? Why did it become a ghost town?

Name _____

Samuel Clemens

A **complex sentence** is made up of one independent clause and one or more dependent clauses. A dependent clause has a subject and a predicate, but it is not a complete thought.

Samuel Clemens moved to the West because he wanted to strike it rich in the mines.
        independent clause   dependent clause

If the dependent clause comes before the subject, use a comma to separate it from the independent clause.

Because he wanted to strike it rich in the mines, Samuel Clemens moved to the West.
        dependent clause   independent clause

Underline the independent clause in each sentence. Underline each dependent clause twice.

1. Samuel Clemens was twenty-five when he and his brother moved to Nevada.

2. They lived in Carson City because Sam's brother worked there for the Territory office.

3. Because he wanted to see the silver mines, Sam traveled to Aurora in 1861.

4. When he returned to Carson City, Sam published articles in a newspaper.

Circle the letter of the complex sentence in this group of sentences.

5. a. Sam tried to strike it rich in the silver mines of Aurora, but he did not find enough silver.

   b. Because he had no money, Sam tried sending some articles, written as letters, to a newspaper called the *Territorial Enterprise* in Virginia City, Nevada.

   c. The letters were published, and Sam was offered a job.

   d. The letters eventually became part of his book, *Roughing It*.

Rewrite this sentence by putting the dependent clause before the independent clause.

6. Samuel Clemens first used the pen name Mark Twain while he worked as a writer in Virginia City, Nevada.

_____

_____

_____

The Fourth of July

In a **simple** sentence or **independent clause**, there is one subject and one predicate. The subject is underlined once, and the predicate twice.

<u>I was born on the Fourth of July</u>.

A **complex** sentence also has an independent clause with one subject and one predicate. The dependent clause is usually part of the predicate and can come before the subject.

<u>My mom likes the fireworks because they are beautiful</u>.

<u>Because they are beautiful</u>, <u>my mom likes the fireworks</u>.

A **compound** sentence has two subjects and two predicates.

<u>I like the bands</u>, <u>and my brother likes the decorations</u>.

Circle the subject and underline the predicate in these sentences.

Simple:

1. I like the Fourth of July.

2. The red, white, and blue colors are so bright.

3. My family and I like the parade the best.

4. The music is so patriotic!

Complex:

5. Even though we like the band music, we also like the barbecue after the parade.

6. We always have to wait our turn when we get to the food stand.

7. I like the hamburgers the best even though I also like hot dogs.

8. After we get our food, we find a nice, shady spot to eat.

Compound:

9. The first song is happy, but the second song sounds sad.

10. It reminds Dad of his Army friends, and Mom puts her arm around him.

11. It's time for the fireworks, and I can hardly wait!

12. We see flashes of blue and yellow, and we hear thunderous booming.

13. It's sad to see the fireworks end, but we can dream about next year.

Autumn Leaves

A **simple** sentence is one independent clause. It has a subject and a predicate and expresses a complete thought.

Autumn is Mom's favorite season.

A **compound** sentence has two independent clauses.

Kimmie and Dex were bored, but they had an idea.

A **complex** sentence has one independent clause and one or more dependent clauses. A dependent clause has a subject and predicate, but it is not a complete thought. The dependent clauses are underlined below.

She sighed as she looked at the leaves littering the yard.

As she looked at the leaves littering the yard, she sighed.

Write an **S** (simple), **CX** (complex), or **C** (compound) to identify each sentence.

_____ 1. Kimmie and Dex decided to rake leaves in the yard to surprise Mom.

_____ 2. They went to the garage to get out the rakes.

_____ 3. Kimmie went to get some trash bags, and Dex picked up sticks.

_____ 4. When Kimmie came back outside, Dex was already raking leaves.

_____ 5. They both worked hard to make a pile of leaves.

_____ 6. As they were raking, Dex noticed the colors of the leaves.

_____ 7. The crimson, golden, and pumpkin-colored leaves were beautiful!

_____ 8. The two children worked hard to rake the leaves into a huge pile.

_____ 9. They set down their rakes, and then they leaped into the leaves.

_____ 10. Mom smiled as she watched her children play in the leaves.

_____ 11. She went outside to help put the leaves into bags.

_____ 12. Because it was a chilly day, Mom made some hot chocolate.

_____ 13. They all sipped the hot chocolate, and they listened to the wind.

_____ 14. The wind tore more leaves off the trees and blew them around.

_____ 15. They all laughed as the yard became covered with leaves again.

You're the author! Write a story about autumn. Use a variety of sentences.

Railroad to the West

Reading only short sentences can be boring. Combine related simple sentences into compound or complex sentences to make writing more interesting.

simple sentence: Some men built tunnels. Other men built bridges.

compound sentence: Some men built tunnels, and other men built bridges.

complex sentence: While some men built tunnels, other men built bridges.

Combine these simple sentences into compound sentences.

1. Railroad owners wanted more tracks. President Lincoln gave them land.

    _____

    _____

2. Many people worked on the railroad to the West. The tracks were finished in 1869.

    _____

    _____

3. The first railroad to the West was done. Other tracks were later built to the West.

    _____

    _____

Combine these simple sentences into complex sentences. (Use the hint word in parentheses.)

4. Men built the railroad to the West. The Civil War was fought. (while)

    _____

    _____

5. Many new settlers moved west. The tracks were finished. (after)

    _____

    _____

6. Building the railroad was very hard. The new tracks helped America. (although)

    _____

    _____

Name _____

Malik the Magician

A **run-on sentence** is two or more sentences that run together without correct punctuation or conjunctions.

run-on:	Malik reached into his hat he pulled out a rabbit.
run-on:	Malik reached into his hat, he pulled out a rabbit.
correct:	Malik reached into his hat. He pulled out a rabbit.
correct:	Malik reached into his hat, and he pulled out a rabbit.

Correct these run-on sentences by writing shorter sentences.

1. The magician waved his wand the girl floated in the air.

   _____

   _____

2. The boy picked a card, Malik already knew which card.

   _____

   _____

3. Malik popped the balloon, a dove flew out of the balloon.

   _____

   _____

Correct these run-on sentences by writing compound sentences. Remember to use a comma and a conjunction in each one.

4. A girl pulled Malik's scarf, a flower popped out of his pocket.

   _____

   _____

5. Malik opened the box the boy was not inside.

   _____

   _____

6. The magician dropped the rope into a bag, a snake slithered out.

   _____

   _____

Name _____

Go Fly a Kite

A **stringy sentence** is one type of run-on sentence. A stringy sentence has too many ideas connected with **or**, **and**, or **but**. You can fix stringy sentences. Use no more than one **or**, **and**, or **but** to connect clauses in each sentence or sentence group.

stringy: Jerome's kite is blue and red, and it has a long tail, and it flies better than any other kite, and it can fly higher than a building.

correct: Jerome's kite is blue and red. It has a long tail. It flies better than any other kite, and it can fly higher than a building.

Correct these stringy sentences by writing three shorter sentences.

1. Caleb's kite is caught in the tree, but he climbs the tree and he gets the kite down.

   _____

   _____

2. The biggest kite belongs to Janelle, but she doesn't know how to fly it very well, and her father helps her.

   _____

   _____

   _____

Correct these stringy sentences by writing two shorter sentences.

3. Chung flies a yellow kite and everyone can see it on a cloudy day and it is cloudy today.

   _____

   _____

   _____

4. I like to fly my kite, but there is not enough wind right now, but I'll try tomorrow.

   _____

   _____

   _____

Name _____

The Mighty Eagle

A **run-on sentence** is two or more sentences that run together without correct punctuation or conjunctions. Fix by writing shorter sentences with correct punctuation.

A **stringy sentence** is one kind of run-on sentence. It has too many ideas connected with **or**, **and**, or **but**. Fix by using no more than one **or**, **and**, or **but** to connect clauses in a sentence group.

Write **run-on** or **stringy** to tell what kind of problem each sentence has. Then either rewrite the sentence or write smaller sentences, with correct punctuation, to fix the problem.

1. _____ Female eagles stay near the nest, male eagles hunt for food.

_____

_____

_____

2. _____ Eagles swoop from the sky, and some eagles pluck fish from the water, but they fly to a safe place to eat.

_____

_____

_____

3. _____ Golden eagles nest on cliffs, and the nests are hard to reach and the eagles can protect their chicks.

_____

_____

_____

4. _____ The bald eagle is the national bird of America, the bald eagle is not really bald.

_____

_____

_____

Check it out! Find more information about eagles. Notice sentence varieties while you read.

Name _____

Dear Detective

Commas are used in the following ways.

in dates:	November 4, 2001
in addresses:	London, England
in a series:	keys, rings, and rocks

in compound sentences before the conjunction:

   I put my keys on a table, and they were gone five minutes later.

in complex sentences when the dependent clause comes before the subject:

   While we were in a meeting, the rock was taken from her desk.

This letter was mailed from Paris to Detective Scott. The person who wrote the letter forgot some commas. Correct the letter by adding the commas. Use the examples above to help you.

 The Nature Museum
24 Louis Boulevard
Paris France

October 6 2001

Dear Detective Scott,

I am writing to ask for your help. During the past three weeks, several small objects have disappeared from the museum. We first noticed the problem on September 23 2001. On that date, Mrs. Kutch's gold ring vanished. We searched the museum but the ring could not be found.

My keys disappeared next. I put my keys on a table and they were gone five minutes later. We looked everywhere.

Kahla was the next victim. She had a beautiful piece of quartz in her office. While we were in a meeting the rock was taken from her desk. This last item was taken on October 3 2001.

We do not know what kind of thief would take keys rings, and rocks. We are worried that more items will disappear. Please help us to solve this crime.

                                        Sincerely,

                                        Pierre Millet

Name _____

The Missing Items

Descriptive words and **details** make writing more exciting and offer additional information to the reader.

beginning sentence:	The ring was gone.
with descriptive words:	The shiny, gold ring with its three rubies was gone.
with detail:	The ring disappeared between noon and 1:00 p.m.
with both:	The shiny, gold ring with its three rubies disappeared between noon and 1:00 p.m.

Detective Scott found some pictures of the missing items. Use the words in the boxed Word Banks to describe the items in the pictures. Write the descriptive words on the lines.

three	valuable	sparkles	velvet

1. Mrs. Kutch's ring is (a) _____.

   The ring is gold and has (b) _____ large rubies.

   The sunlight (c) _____ in the red gems.

   The ring disappeared from its blue (d) _____ case.

parrot	soft	carefully	silver

2. Mr. Millet's keys hang on a long, (a) _____

   chain. The keys are stamped with the Museum's

   (b) _____ design. Mr. Millet

   (c) _____ wipes the keys with a

   (d) _____ cloth to keep them shiny.

smooth	broken	third

3. Kahla collects rocks for the museum. She kept a

   (a) _____ piece of quartz on her desk. The rock's

   (b) _____ sides shine in the light. Her quartz was

   the (c) _____ object to disappear.

Name _____

Bigger and Brighter

Comparing one thing with another is an effective way to paint a picture in the reader's mind. When comparing two items, add an **-er** to the adjective, or describing word.

old —————➤ older

white —————➤ whiter (drop the silent **e** before adding the ending)

silly —————➤ sillier (change the **y** to an **i** before adding the ending)

When comparing three or more items, add an **-est** to the adjective, or describing word.

black ——➤ blackest   wise ——➤ wisest   smelly ——➤ smelliest

Detective Scott looked around the museum and took notes on what he saw. He was in such a hurry that he did not always use the correct comparison words. Circle the comparison words that Detective Scott wrote incorrectly. Then rewrite the correct words on the lines.

1.   The Wood Room has some old wooden carvings. Even oldest than the carvings is a set of wooden dishes used by an ancient culture. The older object in the room is a large piece of petrified wood. Petrified wood is wood that has turned to stone.

   a. _____   b. _____

2.   Next to the Wood Room is a room full of rocks. At first, I thought the larger rock in the room was a geode. A geode is a rock with crystals inside. Then I saw an even biggest piece of shiny marble. I didn't notice the marble at first because a big, red parrot was perched on top of it.

   c. _____   d. _____

3.   The next room had glass cases full of gems. The diamonds were beautiful. There were also several rubies. The brighter ruby was displayed on a glass shelf. I also saw two opals. One was much smallest than the other one, but they were both beautiful.

   e. _____   f. _____

4.   The last room was the noisiest. This was the Bird Room. Even the smaller bird was loud. One bright red parrot swooped over my head. He was biggest than the other parrots. As he flew past me down the hall, one red feather fell to the floor.

   g. _____   h. _____

Name _____

◆◆◆◆◆◆◆◆◆◆◆◆◆◆◆◆◆◆◆◆◆◆◆◆◆◆◆◆◆◆◆◆◆◆◆◆◆

Where Were You?

Make a sentence better by **adding details** and **explanations** to tell **how**, **when**, or **where** something happens.

basic sentence:	Detective Scott searched the museum.
adding how:	Detective Scott searched the museum **carefully**.
adding when:	Detective Scott searched the museum carefully **for two days**.
adding where:	Detective Scott searched **every room and office of the museum carefully** for two days.

◆◆◆◆◆◆◆◆◆◆◆◆◆◆◆◆◆◆◆◆◆◆◆◆◆◆◆◆◆◆◆◆◆◆◆◆◆

Detective Scott is asking the people in the museum questions. Help him by circling the sentences that give all the details and explanations he needs for his notebook. (Hint: the correct sentences for the detective's notebook must tell **how**, **when**, and **where**.)

1. Where was Mr. Millet when the keys disappeared?

    a. Mr. Millet was cleaning a glass case with a cloth.

    b. Mr. Millet was in the Rock Room wiping a glass case.

    c. Mr. Millet spent five minutes in the Rock Room wiping a glass case with a cloth.

2. What was Mrs. Kutch doing when she noticed her ring was missing?

    a. Mrs. Kutch was at her desk sorting through all of her extra paperwork.

    b. Mrs. Kutch was in her office neatly filing her papers after lunch.

    c. Mrs. Kutch worked in the Gem Room until late at night.

3. Where was Kahla when her rock was taken?

    a. Kahla first found her rock when she was on a tour in Spain three years ago.

    b. Kahla spent two hours at a meeting in the Rock Room learning about geodes.

    c. Kahla was busy learning about geodes for two hours.

Write two questions that would help to find out how, when, or where the thefts happened.

4. _____

5. _____

© McGraw-Hill Children's Publishing   23   IF87135 *Building Writing Skills*

Why Did It Happen?

Make a sentence better by telling **why** something happens. This allows a reader to understand the **cause** and the **effect**.

basic sentence: Mr. Millet put his keys on a table.

better sentence: Mr. Millet put his keys on a table so he could clean a glass case.

basic sentence: Mrs. Kutch kept the ring on her desk.

better sentence: Mrs. Kutch kept the ring on her desk because she was going to show it to some friends.

The people at the museum are telling Detective Scott why things happened. Help the detective organize his notes by matching each effect to the correct cause.

Effect

1. Mr. Millet left the Rock Room _____

2. Kahla kept a piece of quartz on her desk _____

3. Mrs. Kutch left her office door open _____

4. Detective Scott looked for clues _____

5. Kahla left her office _____

6. Mr. Millet wrote a letter to Detective Scott _____

7. Mrs. Kutch looked for suspects in the museum _____

8. Detective Scott realized who took the missing items _____

Cause

a. because she was going to show her ring to some friends after lunch.

b. to go get his keys.

c. because he wanted to solve the crime.

d. because it had broken off from a bigger piece of quartz.

e. because she wanted to know who took her ring.

f. because he found an important clue.

g. to go to a meeting about geodes.

h. to ask for help in solving the crimes.

You're the author! Write down the causes and effects from your favorite mystery story.

Name _____

Great Scott!

You can make your sentences **super** sentences by telling **who**, **what**, **where**, **when**, **why**, and **how**.

regular sentence: Kahla walked into the room.

super sentence: Kahla, the museum's rock expert, walked slowly into the meeting room early that morning to discuss the case with Detective Scott.

Detective Scott shared his findings with the people at the museum. Each of his sentences is missing one of the basic elements: **who**, (did) **what**, **where**, **when**, **why**, or **how**. Cross out each boxed element when you see it in the sentence. One word will be left.

1. Mr. Millet, the manager of the Nature Museum, gently set his keys on a table in the Rock Room because he needed to clean one of the glass cases with a cloth.

who	did what	where	when	why	how

2. Mrs. Kutch, the manager of the Gem Room, set the ring on her desk before lunch so that she could show it to some friends.

who	did what	where	when	why	how

3. Kahla, the museum's rock expert, hunted carefully for two days, trying to find her missing piece of quartz.

who	did what	where	when	why	how

4. The naughty thief, who loves shiny objects, left clues in each room during the crimes because this species of thief sheds every season.

who	did what	where	when	why	how

You're the author! Write your own super sentence to tell who, what, where, when, why, and how the missing items were taken from the Nature Museum.

The Main Goal

A **paragraph** is a group of sentences that tells the reader about one main idea.
This is a paragraph:

    The topic sentence tells the main idea of the paragraph. Often, the topic sentence comes first. The rest of the sentences tell more about the idea. These are called supporting sentences. All of the sentences in a paragraph describe one main idea. The first line of the paragraph is indented, which means it is moved in from the left side.

Read each paragraph. Write the letter of the correct main idea from the Idea Bank on the line before each paragraph. Some of the ideas in the Idea Bank will not be used.

____ 1.   Soccer is a popular team sport. A soccer team is made up of eleven people. The four main positions are goalkeeper, defender, midfielder, and forward. A team can only have one goalkeeper, but the other positions can be filled by more players.

____ 2.   Soccer does not need as much equipment as other sports. The soccer ball is the main piece of equipment. Also, each player should have a good pair of shoes with cleats and a pair of shin guards. The goalkeeper often wears padded gloves. The largest piece of equipment is a net called the goal. Each team has a goal.

____ 3.   When playing soccer, the players are not allowed to touch the ball with their hands. They can use their feet, head, legs, or chest to pass the ball down the field to a teammate. When the ball is close to the other team's goal, a player should try to score by kicking the ball past the goalkeeper into the net.

Idea Bank

a.   The equipment needed to play soccer is expensive.

b.   There is not a lot of equipment required to play soccer.

c.   Defenders try to keep the other team from scoring.

d.   Eleven teams can play soccer.

e.   A soccer team is made up of many different positions.

f.   Players must score goals without using their hands to touch the ball.

g.   Scoring a goal is easy if you kick the ball hard.

Check it out! Find a nonfiction book or magazine. Count how many paragraphs there are on one page. Are the paragraphs indented, or is there a blank line between each paragraph?

Name _____

The Windy City

A **paragraph** is a group of sentences that tells the reader about one main idea. If sentences do not support the main idea, they do not belong in the paragraph.

Read each paragraph. Circle the letter of the sentence following the paragraph that tells the main idea. Cross out one sentence in each paragraph that does not support the main idea.

1.   Most people know that Chicago is called the Windy City. People have many theories about this nickname. Some say that a group of people bragged about the city constantly to try to get Chicago chosen as the site for the 1893 World's Fair. People in cities chose school boards, too. A newspaper editor wrote that people shouldn't believe all the claims of "that windy city." The wind was bragging, not breezes! Now you know one possible reason that Chicago is called the Windy City.

   a. Chicago is called the Windy City because people bragged about it too much.

   b. Editors who write about windy cities run their newspapers like businesses.

2.   Chicago is well known for its great fire. The fire swept through the city in 1871. The fire destroyed about one-third of the city. It burned for three days. The homes of more than 90,000 people were burned. More than 250 people were killed. Fires cause a lot of damage all around the world. Nobody knows exactly how the fire started. Some people think a cow kicked over a lantern. Then the lantern started a fire behind someone's house. The lantern fire spread over the dry ground and grew into the fire that became part of Chicago's history.

   a. A cow started the great fire of 1871.

   b. The great fire of 1871 destroyed part of Chicago.

Circle the letters of the sentences that might belong in the second paragraph.

   3. a. Cows should not be allowed in large cities.

      b. Over seventy firemen fought the blaze.

      c. Chicago was rebuilt quickly.

      d. A long dry spell helped the fire to spread quickly.

Name _____

Horses at Work

The main idea of a paragraph is called the **topic**. One sentence usually states the topic. It is called the **topic sentence**. Often, the topic sentence is the first sentence in the paragraph.

Read each unfinished paragraph. Then, circle the best topic sentence to start each paragraph.

1. a. Different horses were used for different kinds of work.

    b. Workhorses had many uses on a farm.

    These animals were slow but very powerful. Early farmers in Europe first used horses to plow their fields. Farmers also used workhorses to pull wagons, so that a load of goods could be taken to market more easily. Finally, the workhorses could drag heavy loads. Farmers cleared their land of trees or large stones with the help of horses. Workhorses made the lives of farmers much easier.

2. a. Arabian horses are different from workhorses.

    b. Horses in the Middle East were not used for farming.

    Arabian horses were first bred in the Middle East. These horses are much smaller than the workhorses found in Europe. Heavy workhorses do not have to move quickly. Arabians are lighter and faster because they were bred for travel. Another difference is that Arabian horses have more stamina. That means they can walk long distances before they need to rest. Workhorses can work very hard for a time, but then they have to rest. Arabian horses and workhorses do different kinds of work.

Write your own topic sentence for this paragraph.

3. _____

   _____

   Spanish explorers brought the first horses to America. These horses were similar to Arabian horses. The Spanish horses may have been the ancestors of the herds of wild horses found in the West. Settlers from England also brought horses to America. Their horses were used for farm work. These are two ways that horses came to America.

Name _____

◆◆◆◆◆◆◆◆◆◆◆◆◆◆◆◆◆◆◆◆◆◆◆◆◆◆◆◆◆◆◆◆◆◆◆◆◆◆

Yeeeehaw!

The main idea of a paragraph is called the **topic**. One sentence usually states the topic. It is called the **topic sentence**. The topic sentence is often the first sentence in the paragraph, but not always.

◆◆◆◆◆◆◆◆◆◆◆◆◆◆◆◆◆◆◆◆◆◆◆◆◆◆◆◆◆◆◆◆◆◆◆◆◆◆

Read each paragraph. Locate the topic sentence in each. Underline the topic sentence.

1.   It's time for excitement! Rodeos began long ago when cowboys wanted to see who was the best at roping and riding. The first unplanned rodeos began in the 1870s and 1880s. Ten years later, rodeos became planned events. Today, many towns host rodeos. Cowboys compete in rope skills and horse racing. They also enter bronco-busting and bull-riding events. From its early days as an informal event, the rodeo has grown into the official sport it is today.

2.   There are many events in a rodeo. Cowboys show their skill at calf roping by tying three of the calf's legs together. The person who ropes the calf in the shortest time wins. Barrel racing is usually a sport for women. A cowgirl rides her horse as fast as possible around three barrels. Cowboys compete in bronc busting, where they try to ride a bronco, a wild horse. Chuck wagon races are well-liked at many rodeos. In this event, horses pull chuck wagons around a track. The fastest team wins.

3.   One of the most exciting events in a rodeo is the bull riding. A brave cowboy sits atop a huge bull. The cowboy wears gloves and chaps for protection. Sometimes, he wears a vest, which helps to protect him in case he falls off the bull. Once the bull charges out of the chute, the cowboy must ride him for eight seconds. If he falls off, he loses. A win can mean a large cash prize or an impressive belt buckle. But, a loss can mean broken bones or even loss of life.

Check it out! Open a nonfiction book. Look for topic sentences in the paragraphs. Are they at the beginning of the paragraphs? On a separate sheet of paper, rewrite one of the paragraphs to change the position of the topic sentence.

◆◆◆◆◆◆◆◆◆◆◆◆◆◆◆◆◆◆◆◆◆◆◆◆◆◆◆◆◆◆◆◆◆◆

Lead Me to Egypt

Sometimes the beginning of a paragraph leads the reader into the selection by offering an **interesting fact** or an **exciting question**. This **lead** is the very beginning of the paragraph. Not every paragraph has a lead.

◆◆◆◆◆◆◆◆◆◆◆◆◆◆◆◆◆◆◆◆◆◆◆◆◆◆◆◆◆◆◆◆◆◆

Read each paragraph. Choose the best lead for each paragraph from the Idea Bank. Write it on the line so it will be the first sentence of the paragraph. Don't forget to indent!

Idea Bank

Pyramids are very large buildings in Egypt.

Some pharaohs wanted large pyramids in which to be buried.

The United States dollar was very important in ancient Egypt.

For 4,500 years, the Great Pyramid of Khufu at Giza was the tallest building in the entire world.

Did you know that ancient Egypt played a part in the design of the U.S. dollar bill?

---

1. _____

   _____

This pyramid was about 480 feet (146 m) high and was 755 feet (230 m) on each side. It has more than two million cut stones, many of which weigh over a ton. The pyramid was the tomb of the great Egyptian pharaoh King Khufu. The pyramid held his mummy and the treasures that the Egyptians believed he would need on his journey into the afterlife. Though not the tallest building any longer, Khufu's tomb, the Great Pyramid of Giza, is still the largest stone building on earth.

2. _____

   _____

A good example of this is the Great Seal of the United States, visible on the back of the dollar bill. Can you see the unfinished pyramid? The pyramid is a sign of strength and permanence. The founding fathers of our country believed that the United States would last like the great pyramids of ancient Egypt. However, because the country would always grow and change, the pyramid was left unfinished in the dollar-bill design.

Check it out! Find a magazine. Look for leads in the very beginning of articles. Did you find facts or questions? What other techniques for leads can you find?

Name _____

Tornado!

A **topic sentence** tells the main idea in a paragraph. A **lead** interests the reader in reading more about the topic. **Supporting sentences** explain more about the main idea. A paragraph often includes at least three key supporting sentences.

Read each topic sentence. Then circle three sentences that support each topic.

1. Tornadoes form in storm clouds when warm air and cold air meet.
    a. They form when the two air masses come together.
    b. States in the Great Plains often have storms.
    c. Warm air rises from the ground, and the storm winds begin to swirl in the sky.
    d. A tornado is extremely dangerous.
    e. Tornadoes over water are called waterspouts.
    f. When the swirling wind reaches down to the ground, it is called a tornado.

2. Tornado Alley lies in the center of the United States.
    a. States with mountains do not have many tornadoes.
    b. Tornadoes can form quickly.
    c. The states in Tornado Alley have open, flat land and many storms.
    d. Tornadoes are likely to occur every year in this part of the country.
    e. A tornado watch means that conditions are right for a tornado to form.
    f. Texas, Oklahoma, Kansas, and Nebraska are all part of Tornado Alley.

3. A tornado came very close to our house last spring.
    a. The sky turned dark, even though it was daytime.
    b. Weather forecasters do not know exactly when a tornado will occur.
    c. Tornadoes sound like trains.
    d. We could hear the wind growling past our windows.
    e. My aunt once saw a tornado while she was driving.
    f. The high winds knocked down our neighbor's tree.

Brrrrrrr! Bears!

The **topic sentence** in a paragraph tells the main idea. **Supporting sentences** explain more about the main idea. Some supporting sentences give examples.

The paragraph below does not give any examples to support the main idea. Choose three examples from the Idea Bank and write them into the paragraph.

Idea Bank

Polar bears eat seals, fish, and bird eggs, among other food.

Polar bears cover their black noses with their paws while they hunt.

Their fur can turn yellowish in the summer.

Their black skin absorbs heat, and their hollow hairs shield their bodies from the cold.

Polar bears can weigh from 550 to 1,800 pounds (250 to 817 kg).

They have wide feet and stiff hairs on their legs that can push against the water.

   Polar bears have everything they need to survive in the frozen Arctic. First, polar bears do not feel the bitter cold like humans do. (1) _____

_____

_____

Second, these marine bears are good swimmers. (2) _____

_____

_____

_____

Finally, they have learned how to hunt in the snowy, white Arctic. (3) _____

_____

_____

_____

There are no other bears that could live so well in the frozen world of the Arctic.

Name _____

Flying Byrd

Transition words help the reader follow the main idea. They can show the **order** or sequence of thoughts. They also show how different ideas are connected.

order: first, second, next, then, finally, last

connection: one, another, often, therefore

Read the paragraph. Underline the transition words. Remember that transition words show the order of thoughts or the connection between ideas.

1.   Richard Evelyn Byrd made many trips to Antarctica. First, he led a two-year mission in 1928. Byrd set up a base called Little America during that trip and made a flight over the South Pole. Next, Byrd returned to Antarctica in 1933. He studied the weather and seasonal patterns. Another trip was made to the frozen south in 1939. He spent a year exploring with his plane. Then, Byrd made a trip in 1946. He flew over the South Pole again during this mission. Finally, in 1955, Byrd made his last trip to Antarctica. He knew more about Antarctica than anyone else at the time.

Write the correct transition word in each blank.

one	then	finally	third	first	because	fourth

2.   Admiral Byrd learned a lot about Antarctica during his trips there.
(a) _____, he mapped and explored over a million square miles of land.
(b) _____, he discovered Marie Byrd Land and the Edsel Ford Mountain Range. (c) _____, he made several flights over the South Pole.
(d) _____ important discovery he made gave us information about the weather patterns in Antarctica. (e) _____, he went on to do research in many other fields of science. Admiral Byrd helped all of us to unlock many of the secrets of Antarctica.

Check it out! Look for transition words in a nonfiction book. Do they show order or do they show connection?

Name _____

Steps to the New World

In some paragraphs, the order or **sequence** of the sentences is very important. Many clues, like **transition words**, help to show the sequence of the sentences.

transition words: first, next, after, then, finally

Christopher Columbus took many steps to get to the New World. The events below are numbered in the correct order. Choose transition words from the box below to write these events into a complete paragraph. The topic sentence is written for you.

1. He studied maps and believed that he could sail west to Asia.

2. He asked the king of Portugal for ships, but the king would not help Columbus.

3. He asked a royal commission in Spain for ships. The commission would not help him.

4. In 1492, King Ferdinand and Queen Isabella, rulers of two Spanish kingdoms, gave him the ships he needed for the voyage.

5. Columbus set sail for Asia, but he discovered the Americas instead.

Christopher Columbus had to work hard before beginning his journey.

Transition Words

Finally,

Another

First,

Often,

Second,

One,

Next,

Then,

Once,

_____
_____
_____
_____
_____
_____
_____
_____
_____
_____
_____
_____

Land! Land!

A paragraph may have a **concluding sentence**. The concluding sentence comes at the end of the paragraph. It reminds the reader of the main idea, summarizes the supporting sentences, gives the reader something to think about, or asks a question.

A sailor on one of Christopher Columbus's ships might have written these paragraphs in a journal. Read each paragraph. Then, circle the best concluding sentence.

1.   I wish I had not signed on to this ship or this dreadful journey. Three days after we left, our mast was damaged. The *Santa María* and the *Niña* helped us get to port for repairs. The *Pinta* was seaworthy again after a few weeks. Now, we sail into the west day after day. I am fearful of the never-ending ocean, savage sea creatures, and even the end of the world.

   a. Why, oh why, did I agree to come on this voyage?

   b. Asia should be just a few days away now.

2.   I think we may convince Columbus to turn back soon. The older sailors have been complaining that he does not know where he is going. Captain Pinzón spoke with Columbus two days ago, and our three ships changed direction to the south-west. Rumor has it that we may try this heading for a few days and then turn back.

   a. I still have faith that Columbus will find a way to the East.

   b. Surely, Columbus knows by now that this quest is hopeless.

Write your own concluding sentence for this entry.

3.   We are near land! First, Señor Cerdá saw a large piece of driftwood yesterday afternoon. Captain Pinzón said that since the wood was not smooth, it could not have been in the water for long. Then, this morning, the lookout on the *Santa María* said he saw some birds.

_____

_____

_____

_____

You're the author! Write your own journal about a journey. Come to a conclusion about whether or not it was a good idea to go on the trip.

Name _____

Let Me Explain

A paragraph may have a **concluding sentence**. This sentence comes at the end of the paragraph. It reminds the reader of the main idea, summarizes the supporting sentences, gives the reader something to think about, or asks a question.

Circle the letter of the best concluding sentence for these paragraphs.

1.   This year, I will do things differently. I will exercise three times a week. I could run, play racquetball, or swim. I plan to keep my room clean. If I put away my clothes every night, the rest will be easy! The last thing I will do is get my homework done. I want to get better grades, and I know that finishing homework on time will help.

   a. I will work hard on my homework all year.

   b. I will do all these things, and have a wonderful year!

   c. Another thing I will do is finish my chores.

2.   Of all the rooms in my house, I spend the most time in the kitchen. Everything important happens there. For example, it's where Mom told us we were going to Hawaii. Mom puts up our best drawings on the refrigerator. It's like a family art gallery! I also spend so much time in the kitchen because my mom is the best cook ever. The air is often filled with the aroma of bacon, cookies, or home-baked bread.

   a. My bedroom is another wonderful room in our house.

   b. I wonder if every family's kitchen is as important as ours.

   c. My house is a wonderful place to live!

3.   Other people have pets they love, but my dog, Princess, is the sweetest dog on earth. She never barks at me. She only barks at strangers, which makes her a good watchdog. Another reason Princess is great is that she is nice to other dogs. She never growls, and she stays by my side during our walks. Finally, Princess always comes when I call her. She runs like the wind to get to me, and then she sits so I can pat her on the head.

   a. I feel so lucky to have such a good dog for a pet.

   b. Princess is very smart, and she learns tricks easily.

   c. I think dogs make the best possible pets.

Name _____

Computers and Homework

An **expository paragraph** gives information or explains something. A paragraph often includes at least three key supporting sentences. Telling more about those ideas makes the paragraph stronger and more complete.

You've been given an assignment to write a paragraph about the different ways a computer is used for homework. Read the topic sentence and the concluding sentence.

Topic sentence: Today, many students use the computer to help with their homework.

Concluding sentence: Doing homework on the computer prepares students for life beyond school.

Now circle three sentences from the list to support the main idea.

1. Students often type their papers on the computer.

2. Students aren't the only ones who use computers to do work at home.

3. Equally important, students can use the computer to research topics for class.

4. Finally, the computer can be used to create presentations for class.

5. One example is when a computer is used to track spending.

6. My best friend and I really love to try out new computer games.

7. Before computers, people used typewriters and carbon paper to do reports.

Next, match each sentence you chose above to the sentence below that tells more about it. Write the numbers of the sentences in the blanks.

a. This teaches students about keyboarding and printing. _____

b. The Internet is a great tool for research. _____

c. Typewritten work was hard to correct and change. _____

d. Some presentation software can even add graphics and sound. _____

e. Adults use computers for office work, bill paying, and writing. _____

f. Every year, computer games get more detailed and fun. _____

g. My father uses our computer to help him do taxes. _____

You're the author! On a separate piece of paper, write out the paragraph you've just created on this page. Add more details or more supporting sentences.

Name _____

My Brother's Shoes

Expository writing gives information or explains something. Before writing an expository piece, write down your ideas, and then plan what you will write. **Plans** are used to put ideas in order. Write out topic and concluding sentences. Other parts of the plan do not need to be written in complete sentences.

Here are some ideas for writing an expository paragraph. Cross out any ideas that do not belong. Then, put the ideas in the plan with related topics grouped together. The transition words will help you with the order.

Ideas	
a. smelly mold growing inside them	f. brother is in third grade
b. third—shoelaces are torn	g. first—pink, bubble gum on the side
c. gum is covered with dirt	h. too short to tie
d. t-shirt is filthy, too	i. second—they stink!
e. My brother's shoes are disgusting.	j. It's a good thing Mom is taking him to buy new shoes today!

1. topic sentence: _____

    _____

2. a. first idea: _____

    b. tell more: _____

3. a. second idea: _____

    b. tell more: _____

4. a. third idea: _____

    b. tell more: _____

5. concluding sentence: _____

    _____

You're the author! Write a paragraph using your plan from this page.

Name _____

Komodo Dragons

Paragraphs are separated by indentation. A new paragraph should begin when there is a new main idea. To **indent** means to move the first line of the paragraph in from the left side. **The beginning of this paragraph is indented.** This tells the reader that there is a new topic or idea.

Oops! There are three paragraphs below, but the scientist who wrote about the Komodo dragon forgot to indent to show where the paragraphs begin. Put an X on each line to show where a new idea begins. That is where a new paragraph should start.

a. _____ The Komodo dragon is the largest living lizard in the world. It has a long neck and a tapered head. It has very strong legs and a long, muscular tail. b._____ Komodo dragons grow up to thirty-three feet (10 m) long and can weigh up to 300 pounds (136 kg)! It is possible for these giant lizards to live for a hundred years. c._____ This huge lizard is a dangerous predator. Being a fast runner, the Komodo dragon catches and eats deer, pigs, wild boars, and other animals. It may also feed on dead animals that it finds. d. _____ A bite from this lizard could be deadly to a human due to bacteria that Komodo dragons have in their mouths. e._____ Komodo dragons live on Komodo Island and a few other islands in Indonesia. Now, the dragons are protected because there are not many of them left. f. _____ About 1,000 live on Komodo Island in Komodo Island National Park. More dragons live on islands nearby.

Check it out! Look in any nonfiction book or magazine. Are the paragraphs indented, or is a line skipped to show where a new paragraph begins? Both methods are common in books and magazines to show when the main idea changes.

The Iditarod

Paragraphs are separated by **indentation**. To indent means to move the first line of the paragraph in from the left side. This tells the reader that there is a new topic or idea.

This passage is written as one paragraph, even though there is more than one topic. Rewrite the passage, using another piece of paper if necessary. Indent for each new paragraph.

The Iditarod Trail Sled Dog Race began in 1973. The race runs from Anchorage to Nome, Alaska. It covers 1,049 miles (1,688 km) and lasts about nine days. In the early 1900s, the town of Iditarod was a gold rush town, halfway between Anchorage and Nome. Dog sleds were used for travel to Iditarod. Now, it is a ghost town. Today, the Iditarod Trail is used for sport: athletes and dogs against the environment. Every March, people test their endurance in the race; one such person was author Gary Paulsen. He later used the experience in a novel. The Iditarod has become an Alaskan tradition.

Name _____

Introducing the Incas

An **expository paragraph** gives information or explains something. One type of expository writing is an **informative paragraph**. It offers information.

Cross out the sentences that do not belong in an **informative paragraph** about the Incan empire in South America. Use the remaining sentences to write an informative paragraph. Remember that a paragraph has a topic and a concluding sentence.

a. The Incas built an empire in South America.

b. You should go to see the Incan ruins.

c. They were finally defeated by Spanish explorers in search of gold.

d. Because of the steep mountains, crops were hard to grow.

e. More than nine million people lived in the Inca Empire.

f. They lived in an area that stretched from the Andes to the Amazon.

g. The Incas, Mayans, and Aztecs all had large empires.

h. The Incas ruled for over two hundred years.

i. A young boy named Manco wanted to be a great warrior.

j. The word *ayllu* means clan or family.

_____

_____

_____

_____

_____

_____

_____

_____

_____

_____

_____

Name _____

The Incas and Us

Expository writing gives information or explains something. A paragraph that tells how things are the same or different is called a **compare-and-contrast** paragraph.

Circle the sentences that belong in a compare-and-contrast paragraph.

1. Although the Incas lived five hundred years ago, there are many similarities between them and North Americans in the last century.

2. Incas were ruled by a royal family, while North Americans had elected officials.

3. Incas and North Americans were both able to perform surgery.

4. Both cultures had farmers, but the majority of Incas were farmers.

5. In 1532, the Spanish explorers conquered the Incas.

6. Leaders of both cultures collected taxes for roads, bridges, and public buildings.

7. Incas spoke Quechuan, but they did not have a written language like English.

8. Some of the Incas were experts in making gold objects.

9. Both cultures invented new technologies to make people's lives better.

A Venn diagram is used to show how things are the same or different. Write the letters of the ideas in the Venn diagram where they belong. The numbered sentences above will help you.

a. had no written language

b. ruled by elected leaders

c. some farmers

d. ruled by a royal family

e. mostly farmers

f. invented new technologies

g. knew how to use surgery to save lives

h. had written language

i. governments collected taxes

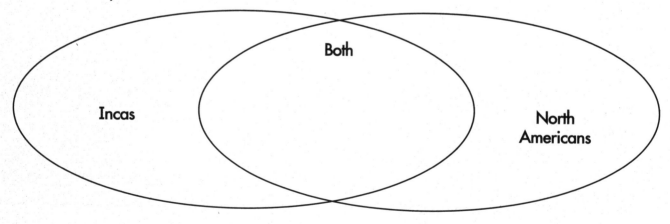

Name _____

Picture This

Expository writing gives information or explains something. A **descriptive paragraph** is expository writing that paints a picture in the reader's mind. Using all five senses—sight, sound, smell, taste, and touch—to describe something adds great interest to a paragraph.

Read the descriptive paragraph about an Incan village. In the blanks below, write the ways the different things in the village are described. Next, write either **sight**, **sound**, **smell**, **taste**, or **touch** to tell which sense the writer used. A hint is given for each blank.

Have you ever wondered what a typical Incan village was like? Picture this. Huge, snow-capped mountains tower over a small cluster of huts. The small, brown, grass-roofed huts in the village are made out of dried mud, called *adobe*. A cold blast of air flows down the mountains and blusters through the village. The rough barking of the dogs and the rumbling bray of the llamas can be heard in every hut. A bitter-corn scent drifts from the clay jugs of *chicha*, a strong drink made from corn. At midday, you might get to taste some guinea-pig stew. This spicy, nutritious stew was made with potatoes, chilies, herbs, and guinea pigs. Heavy, woolen blankets, as rough as stiff, dry grass, might be hanging over stools or fences to dry. In the evening, the distant cries of birds echo in the mountains. Does this sound like a beautiful place to live, or a harsh way of life?

		description	sense
1.	(mountains)	_____	_____
2.	(huts)	_____	_____
3.	(air)	_____	_____
4.	(llamas)	_____	_____
5.	(chicha jugs)	_____	_____
6.	(stew)	_____	_____
7.	(blankets)	_____	_____
8.	(birds)	_____	_____

You're the author! Write a descriptive paragraph about your room. Include each of the five senses. Remember that a paragraph must have a topic sentence and a concluding sentence.

Problems for the Incas

An **expository paragraph** gives information or explains something. An expository paragraph that offers one or more solutions to a specific problem is called a **problem/solution paragraph**.

The paragraph below is about solutions to a problem. It is not a complete problem/solution paragraph because it does not describe the problem. Circle the letters of the two best problem statements. Write your favorite of the two on the line.

1. a. The steep, rocky mountains did not allow them to grow enough food.

    b. Their empire was growing too large.

    c. They needed to find better ways to raise animals to feed their people.

    d. How could they grow food on the sides of mountains?

The Incas faced a serious problem as their empire grew.

_____

_____

_____

First, the Incas built large, stone terraces, which looked like steps in the sides of the mountains. These terraces formed small fields that allowed the Incas to grow crops. Then, the Incas built complex canals to bring water to the fields. This meant they could grow crops even when there was not enough rain. Finally, large granaries, or grain houses, were built to store extra food. During years that were bad for growing food, the Incas had enough stored supplies to survive. With these solutions, the Incas were able to grow enough food for their nine million people.

Write an idea that might solve the following problem for the Incas:

2. The Incas had many small villages scattered across their land. They needed a way to send messages and news to all of the people in their empire. Since there were no telephones or television, they found other solutions.

_____

_____

       IF87135 *Building Writing Skills*

Name _____

Next Stop, Machu Picchu

Expository writing gives information or explains something. The expository **how-to paragraph** explains the steps involved in how to do something. The how-to paragraph informs the reader what materials will be needed. Also, the paragraph gives directions in a specific order.

The following paragraph describes how to get to Machu Picchu, an ancient Incan city that is now a ruin. Make a list of the things you will need to take on this trip. Then, mark your way on the map by drawing lines that show what the paragraph tells you to do.

     Getting to Machu Picchu, the great Incan ruin, is not easy. You will need two airline tickets; a train ticket to the trailhead; a backpack; and camping supplies. First, you need to fly to the city of Lima in Peru. Then, you take a short flight from Lima to Cusco. Next, you must take a train from Cusco to the trailhead in Chilca, near Abancay. Finally, when you reach the Salcantay trailhead in Chilca, you are ready to begin hiking. You will walk the Salcantay Trail for two to six days, camping along the way, before you reach Machu Picchu. After all that travel, you will finally stand in the ancient city of the Incas.

Things I Need

1. _____
   _____
   _____
2. _____
   _____
   _____
3. _____
   _____
4. _____
   _____
   _____

You're the author! Write directions telling someone how to ride a bike. Remember to include the equipment that the person will need.

Name _____

Let's Go!

Expository writing gives information or explains something. In a **persuasive paragraph**, one kind of expository writing, the writer tries to talk the reader into something.

Here is a list of thoughts about going to Machu Picchu for vacation. Some of the thoughts are reasons for going to Machu Picchu. Some are reasons against going to Machu Picchu. Write the word **for** or **against** in front of each thought.

_____ 1. takes a long time to get there

_____ 2. could learn some fascinating history

_____ 3. might cost too much

_____ 4. cannot speak the language there

_____ 5. adventure of a lifetime

_____ 6. should not drink the water there

_____ 7. could learn about new people

_____ 8. hike through gorgeous mountains

_____ 9. see things you've never seen before

Use the strongest three "for" reasons to write a persuasive paragraph. Remember, a persuasive paragraph tries to talk someone into doing something. The topic sentence and concluding sentence are done for you.

I think there are many good reasons to go to Machu Picchu for vacation this year.

_____

_____

_____

_____

_____

_____

_____

_____

_____

If we don't go to Machu Picchu, we're cheating ourselves out of a great vacation!

Name _____

The End of the Incas

Expository writing gives information or explains something. A **cause-and-effect paragraph** explains why something happened. A **cause** is something that makes something else happen. An **effect** happens because of the cause.

Match each cause to its effect.

Cause	**Effect**
1. _____ The Inca Indians did not have guns.	a. The Spanish attacked the Incas for their gold.
2. _____ The Incas' power and wealth had made them famous among other tribes in the region.	b. The Spanish explorers were able to easily defeat the Incas with their troops and muskets.
3. _____ The Incas showed the Spanish their gold jewelry and art.	c. The Incas thought the light-skinned Spaniards were sent from the sun god.
4. _____ The Spanish explorers had light-colored skin.	d. Other tribes in South America told the Spanish explorers about the wealth of the great empire in the west, the Incas.
5. _____ The Spanish wanted to conquer the people who ruled the region and who had the most wealth.	e. So, the explorers began to search for the Incas.

Read this cause-and-effect paragraph. Underline the causes and circle the effects.

A long time with no rain, called a drought, could cause a serious problem for the Incas. When there was a drought, not as much food could be grown. If there was not enough food, the *ayllus*, or families, could barely feed themselves. So when there was no extra food, the leaders could not tax the people. Without the tax, the Incas could not afford to build more roads or bridges, and they could not repair damaged roads either.

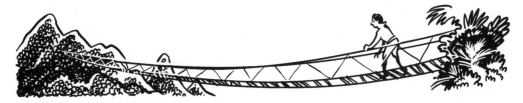

You're the author! Choose causes and effects from items 1–5 and a–e to write a cause-and-effect paragraph about the end of the Incan empire.

                   IF87135 *Building Writing Skills*

descriptive paragraphs

Name _____

The Concert

Expository writing gives information or explains something. A **descriptive paragraph** is an expository paragraph that paints a picture in the reader's mind. Using all five senses—sight, sound, smell, taste, and touch—to describe something adds great interest to a paragraph.

Write down the sense—**sight, sound, smell, taste,** or **touch**—that best describes each item. Then write words or phrases to show how that sense describes the item. The first one is done for you.

	thing	sense	description
1.	lemonade	taste	sweet, lip-puckering, refreshing, cold
2.	instruments		
3.	music		
4.	lights		
5.	seats		
6.	costumes		
7.	perfume		
8.	people		

Use some of your descriptions above to write a paragraph about a concert. Remember to "paint a picture" for your reader by using different senses. Don't forget to indent!

_____
_____
_____
_____
_____
_____
_____
_____
_____
_____

Name _____

You Need A Pencil

Expository writing gives information or explains something. A **how-to** paragraph is an expository paragraph explaining the steps involved in how to do something. The how-to paragraph tells the reader what materials will be needed and gives directions in a specific order.

Read the how-to paragraphs below. Circle the letter that tells what error, if any, was made.

1.   Keeping in touch with your grandpa or favorite aunt is easy. All you need is paper, a pencil, an envelope, and a stamp. Write the address on the envelope, and put a stamp in the upper right-hand corner. Put your written letter inside the envelope. Next, lick the envelope and press it closed. Finally, you are ready to mail your letter. Write about the things that are special to you and your aunt or grandpa in your letter. You won't have to wait long before you'll have an answer!

   a. The writer forgot to tell what materials are needed.

   b. The how-to steps were not in the right order.

   c. There were too many extra details.

   d. This how-to paragraph is correct.

2.   Do you like to draw? If so, you can make a cartoon. First, imagine a character and something for it to do. Pick a character that you like to draw. Next, draw the character on the first page of the pad. Then, draw the character on the following pages, but draw it in a slightly different position on each page. When you are done, go back to the first page and flip through the pages quickly. Your character will come to life as the pages flip.

   a. The writer forgot to tell what materials are needed.

   b. The how-to steps were not in the right order.

   c. There were too many extra details.

   d. This how-to paragraph is correct.

You're the author! Write a how-to paragraph telling how to make a glass of chocolate milk. Remember to indent your paragraph and use the correct how-to paragraph form.

Name _____

Penguins and Puffins

Expository writing gives information or explains something. An expository paragraph that tells how things are the same or different is called a **compare-and-contrast** paragraph.

Read each paragraph. Make a list of three things that are the same about penguins and puffins. Then, make a list of three things that are different.

Penguins

The unique-looking penguin is a sea bird that is native to the waters of the southern hemisphere. Penguins cannot fly, but they are excellent swimmers. Seventeen types of penguins have been discovered. Most penguins have black feathers in back and white feathers on the fronts of their bodies. Penguins spend most of their time out at sea but come to land to raise their young. Mother penguins lay one or two eggs each season.

Puffins

Puffins are a kind of sea bird native to the cold waters of the northern hemisphere. Puffins can fly, but not very well. Three types of puffins have been discovered. Their bodies are covered with black-and-white or all-black feathers. Puffins' bills are large and shaped like triangles. These birds swim well and eat fish. Puffins spend most of their time out at sea but come to land to raise their young. Mother puffins lay only one egg each season.

1. **how penguins and puffins are the same**

  a. _____

     _____

     _____

  b. _____

     _____

     _____

  c. _____

     _____

     _____

2. **how penguins and puffins are different**

  a. _____

     _____

     _____

  b. _____

     _____

     _____

  c. _____

     _____

     _____

You're the author! On a separate sheet of paper, write a compare-and-contrast paragraph about puffins and penguins. Use the paragraphs and your lists from above to help you.

Name _____

Can I Keep It?

Expository writing gives information or explains something. In a **persuasive paragraph**, one kind of expository writing, the writer tries to persuade the reader to do something or to think in a certain way. Often, a persuasive paragraph tries to deal with the reader's doubts.

A dog you found in an empty field follows you home. Your mother has some concerns about keeping the dog. Read each concern. Circle the letter of the idea that best addresses each concern and might persuade your mother that it is not a problem.

1. "You cannot keep the dog because it might belong to someone else."

   a. I will put up signs to check around the neighborhood for a possible owner.

   b. It does not have a nametag or a collar, and I did not find it near a house.

   c. It probably does not belong to anybody else.

2. "You cannot keep the dog because you do not know how to take care of it."

   a. You can take care of it, and I'll just play with it.

   b. Taking care of a dog is easy.

   c. I'll go to the pet store and ask them how to take care of a dog.

3. "You cannot keep the dog because it will make the whole house smell."

   a. It does not smell any worse than my brother's shoes.

   b. I will spray the house whenever it smells bad.

   c. The dog can live in a doghouse in the backyard.

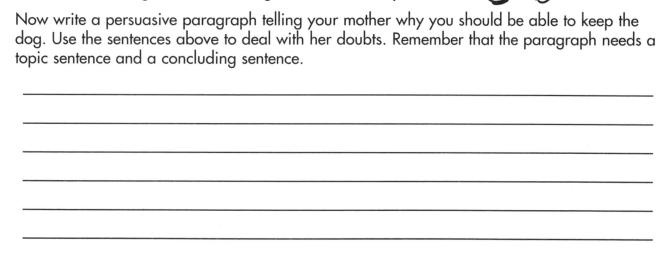

Now write a persuasive paragraph telling your mother why you should be able to keep the dog. Use the sentences above to deal with her doubts. Remember that the paragraph needs a topic sentence and a concluding sentence.

_____

_____

_____

_____

_____

_____

◆◇◆

Scuba Diving

When writing **more than one paragraph about a single subject**, the first paragraph introduces the topic, just like the topic sentence in a paragraph. Supporting sentences develop, or tell more, about the topic. There is no concluding sentence because the writer has more ideas.

The next paragraph begins with a topic sentence that has a transition from the first paragraph to the next. Transitions help the reader follow the main idea. They show the order of events or how different ideas are connected. Supporting sentences develop the new idea.

The last paragraph concludes the writing. Like a concluding sentence, it needs to remind the reader of the topic or leave the reader with something to think about. This paragraph needs to contain the concluding sentence.

◆◇◆

Read the three-paragraph essay. Then, choose which of the single paragraphs that follow it (a, b, or c) was expanded to create the essay.

Wave of the Future

Diving is a very popular sport. Many people train for scuba diving every year. Scuba trainers believe that over six million people have been trained. These people dive for many different reasons.

Many people simply want to explore the beauty under the sea. They dive to see the brilliant colors and striking shapes. Some want to watch the slow-motion dance of a sea turtle or the playful sport of dolphins. These divers enjoy the scenery of the sea.

Other people dive for thrill and adventure. They want to explore underwater caves or shipwrecks. These people like to dive in places no one else has ever been. Both groups, the scenery-viewers and the adventurers, help to make diving a sport that is sure to keep growing in the future.

a.   Many people join in the sport of diving every year. They are interested in the many different activities under the water. Some people seek beauty, while others look for adventure. No wonder this sport is growing so quickly.

b.   Diving is a popular hobby. Many people are interested in the kingdom under the sea. Some divers stay in the shallow water with a snorkel. This lets them explore without going completely under the water. Snorkeling gives the thrill of diving without the need for scuba-diving equipment. More people begin snorkeling every year.

c.   Scuba divers live thrilling lives. They get to see some of the most beautiful places in the world. Some people take pictures or videos under the water. Others search for treasure in old shipwrecks. A few even explore caves under the ocean. Would you like to visit the exciting world under the sea?

Name _____

To Test or Not to Test

A **five-paragraph essay** is like a stretched-out paragraph. The topic sentence stretches to the first paragraph, the **introduction**. The key supporting sentences develop the ideas in the body, or **middle paragraphs** of the essay. The concluding sentence becomes the last paragraph, or **conclusion**.

paragraph		**essay**
topic sentence	⟶	introduction
key supporting sentences	⟶	body paragraphs
concluding sentence	⟶	conclusion

Read the five-paragraph essay. Underline the topic sentences in each paragraph and the concluding sentence at the end of the essay.

Have you ever wondered why you have to take state tests? State tests try to find out if the educational system is working as it should. These tests may seem like extra work. However, they are very important to many people, and mainly to you, the student.

First, it is vital to know if students are learning what is being taught. The test can show areas where a student or a class needs extra help. Teachers need to know how well each student learned the lessons.

Also, these tests may show whether a school is teaching the right skills in the right way. Schools sometimes need to alter how they teach by changing methods or using different vocabulary. Testing is a good way to find out if the students understand the information they are given.

Another reason to test is so each state can measure how well all of the schools are doing. The state compares all the schools in the state. This data is used to make changes to the schools or districts.

These tests may help your classes improve. A better school system benefits you, the student. Used well, testing can be helpful.

Write a single paragraph using the sentences you underlined.

_____

_____

_____

_____

_____

Name _____

Nine Lives

A **narrative** tells a story. A story can be made up or about real life.
Expository writing gives information or explains something.

Write the letter **N** for narrative on the line by a story paragraph. Write **E** for expository on the line by a paragraph that gives information or explains something.

_____ 1.   Cats were first kept as pets in 2500 B.C. by the Egyptians. These first house cats were probably a type of wildcat called a Caffre cat. The idea of keeping a cat as a pet spread to Europe. Caffre cats were brought to Europe and are the ancestors of many of the modern cat breeds.

_____ 2.   Samantha, the lightning cat, tensed all her muscles. She jumped in an instant—just a blur to the eyes. A second later, she was across the room chewing on a plant. Then, again, just a flash of fur, and she was upstairs sleeping on the bed. No one could figure out how she moved so quickly.

_____ 3.   "Order! Order!" called Lord Charles, the old Persian. All the other cats, except for Ling, settled down into their seats. Ling was a Siamese cat, and she was feisty. She paraded around the room with her head high, hoping every-one would notice her shiny beige coat. "Ling, sit down," meowed Lord Charles. She slowly waltzed to her seat.

_____ 4.   The image of the cat has long been adored by people. The earliest paintings and sculptures of cats can be found in Egyptian tombs. Cats appear on both Greek and Roman coins. The Irish *Book of Kells* from the eighth century has images of cats and kittens. Even Leonardo da Vinci drew cats and put them in his paintings.

_____ 5.   Rags, a very tattered and dirty cat, stood up and shook his head. He tried to remember what had happened. There was a loud screech and two bright lights. The lights rushed quickly toward him. Right before the lights touched him, a great wind swept him out of the way. He was alive. But, somehow he felt lighter, as if something special had been taken from him. A chill seeped through his thinning fur.

◆◆◆◆◆◆◆◆◆◆◆◆◆◆◆◆◆◆◆◆◆◆◆◆◆◆◆◆◆◆◆◆◆◆◆

Parts

A **narrative** is a story. Like expository writing, a story has a **beginning** (introduction), a **middle** (body), and an **end** (conclusion).

narrative		expository
beginning	⟶	introduction
middle	⟶	body
end	⟶	conclusion

◆◆◆◆◆◆◆◆◆◆◆◆◆◆◆◆◆◆◆◆◆◆◆◆◆◆◆◆◆◆◆◆◆◆◆

Read the following parts of stories. Write **beginning**, **middle**, or **end** by each part to show where it belongs in a story.

1. _____ HB-68, the world's first Health-Bot, scanned the landscape. Its long-distance sensor watched a small column of smoke, all that was left of Dr. Seau's lab. After everything that had happened, this looked like the end. A safety program began to shut down HB-68. The bot closed its sensors and was still at last.

2. _____ Maya and Finney met at the bridge, like they did every Saturday. But tonight felt different. The cold moon glared brightly. It seemed to be watching them closely, as if some strange magic was about to begin. That's when Finney saw the shadow on the other side of the river.

3. _____ The sail puffed out its chest and stood strong against the wind. The mast groaned. The first mate carefully looked over the repairs. He smiled and shouted, "She'll be able to fight a storm, Captain." He knew they would go on with their important journey.

4. _____ Carlos Berda couldn't help it. A huge smile crawled across his face. They would not let him into medical school. They had refused to share their research. Even his own company had told him that his experiment would fail. Now he held the award close to his chest. Everyone who had told him "No" was asking for his research. He had done it!

5. _____ After the rain stopped, Owl stepped from his hollow tree onto the large branch. The forest looked messy from too much rain. Puddles and patches of brown mud dotted the ground. He saw no sign of his friends. He would check on them soon. First, he had to go finish things with the Badger.

6. _____ The bus pulled into the parking lot, and out stepped J.T. Hopper. He was short, with long, dusty, red hair smoothed against his head. He looked harmless, but the other boys knew better. The guards had warned them not to get in J.T.'s way, especially not on his first day.

Name _____

In the Beginning

The **setting** is when and where a story takes place.

Read these story beginnings. Match each story beginning to when and where it takes place. Write the letters and Roman numerals on the lines. The first one is done for you.

Story Beginning

1. __d, V__   She heard the noise again. It sounded very loud in the silent stillness of a morning in the farmland.

2. _____   The water was lapping softly on the side of the wooden ship. The hurricane had passed, and they were alive!

3. _____   The neon lights flashed brightly. The city sounds were all around him. Should he take the subway, or would it be better to walk? He needed to arrive by 6:00 p.m. at the latest.

4. _____   Victoria had family in the Oregon Territory. She wanted desperately to see them. Summer on the trail was so hard!

5. _____   Tiny Toaster looked across the room. The kitchen was so scary in the dark. Even the little light over the stove did not help tonight. Tiny wrapped his cord around himself. He always felt safer that way.

6. _____   "Zoooom!" The Starship Feebelot whizzed past the small hurricane planet. It was Nilon Omniblat's birthday.

When

a. summer

b. on his birthday

c. about 5:45 pm

d. ~~morning~~

e. at night

f. after the hurricane

Where

I. in the kitchen

II. in the city

III. on the Oregon trail

IV. in space

V. ~~in the country~~

VI. on the ocean

You're the author! Write your own story beginning. Remember to show when and where the story takes place so readers will understand your setting.

Name _____

Fillmore Ice Boys

Characters are the people, animals, or things that do or say things in a story. Writers sometimes describe what the characters look like. More often, they tell how the characters think, act, and talk.

Read the passage. In the blanks below, write all the ways the writer describes each character.

The Fillmore Ice Boys gathered at their usual place, Reggie's tree house. Reggie was the leader of the club for two reasons. First, the tree house was in his backyard. Second, he had stayed in the ice water a minute longer than anyone else. He was tall with questioning eyes. He was not the smartest or the toughest, but he never gave up.

Oloognik was in the club, too. In fact, he was the reason the boys formed the club. He told stories about the days he had lived in Alaska. He had fallen into the freezing water of the Arctic Ocean twice while hunting. Oloog was a little chubby. He had a memorable way of looking at someone with his dark eyes. It seemed like he could see right through you to your heart. He was the kindest boy in the school.

The third boy to join the club was Pedro, but the others called him Chilly. He never wanted to go into the ice water. And when he found he had to stay in the water for at least a minute, he had started shivering. Oloog often said that Chilly had been shivering ever since. Chilly was short, with a long, happy face. His movements were small and quick, like a bird's.

The last of the Fillmore Ice Boys was Ted. He was the loudest member of the club. His super-short hair made his head look shiny. Ted was always excited about something, and he couldn't wait to tell about it. Then he would speak as fast as the wind. The whole time he was in the ice water, he never stopped telling the others about his trip down the Mississippi River. "I was just like Tom Sawyer," he kept saying.

		how the character looks	how the character thinks, acts, or talks
1.	Reggie	_____	_____
2.	Oloog	_____	_____
3.	Chilly	_____	_____
4.	Ted	_____	_____

Name _____

Let Me Introduce You

Characters can be people, animals, or things. A story tells what the characters do. We get to know the characters by how they think, act, and talk.

Read each passage. Then circle the letter of the thing the character might do, based on your understanding of the information in the passage.

1.   Everyone expects Shireen to know the answers because she studies so hard. She loves music, too. She practices piano every day. Shireen is always smiling. She is kind and polite to people.

   Shireen is invited to an overnight party on Friday at her friend's house. Everyone plans to stay up all night. The only problem is that Shireen has a piano recital on Saturday morning. She wants to do well. What will she do?

   a. She will go to the party for the evening, but not stay the night.

   b. She tells her friend she does not want to go to the party.

   c. She will go to the party and stay up all night with her friends.

2.   Brandon threw the doll down the laundry chute and banged the door shut. He would get even with Meghan, his sister. Mom and Dad couldn't make him be nice to her. He kicked the wall and muttered to himself.

   "Brandon!" called his mother. "Meghan is crying. She says you took her doll. Do you know where it is?"

   What does Brandon say?

   a. "Yes, I took the doll because I am mad at Meghan."

   b. "Gosh, Mom, I don't know."

   c. "How would I know what happened to her stupid doll?"

3.   The wise and fair king of beasts was called upon to help the monkeys and the giraffes come to an agreement. The monkeys said that all the leaves on the trees belonged to them. The giraffes believed that the leaves within their reach should be their food to eat.

   How does the king of beasts help them decide what to do?

   _____

   _____

You're the author! Create your own special character. What would he or she do in each of the situations above? How do you know?

Name _____

◆◆◆

Conflicting Stories

Every story has a **conflict**. The conflict is the main character's problem or a problem in which he or she is involved. The story is about finding a solution to that problem.

◆◆◆

Read the beginning of these stories. Then, circle the letter of the sentence that best describes the **conflict**.

1.   Old Casper Munfeld listened to the tick of the grandfather clock. Tick. Tick. Tick. The clock, with its gilded face, was worth a fortune. But it seemed worthless now, ticking away in the huge house. Munfeld had made millions by being a tough businessman. He treated money better than he had treated people. Now that his business years were over, he had no one to share his success. There was a hole in his life.

   a. Casper Munfeld is lonely and needs people in his life.

   b. Mr. Munfeld should have lived his life differently by taking care of people.

   c. Casper Munfeld's house is too big for just one person.

2.   The sleek steamer slipped through the quiet night. Only the churning engines and the surging water broke the silence. Out in the inky black, two women struggled in a small boat. They had no way to signal the huge ship. Their only hope of survival was to get out of the steamer's path. Danielle was better with the oars, and she rowed as hard as she could. Kimiko tried to cheer her on while she bailed some of the water out of the boat with her purse.

   a. The steamer is traveling too fast.

   b. Danielle and Kimiko need someone to help them row.

   c. Danielle and Kimiko are struggling to get out of the way of a steamer.

Write a complete sentence to describe the conflict in this story beginning.

3.   Shanna and Kylie walked past another street they did not know. The sun was beginning to set, and the two girls were near a dangerous part of the city. Some loud people in an empty lot scared them. The girls hurried past. Shanna thought they should walk toward the highway, but Kylie did not want to leave this street. While they argued, the shadows grew.

   _____

   _____

You're the author! Write a sentence to describe the main conflict in your favorite story.

Name _____

Cheeser and the Cat

The **plot** is the action, or series of events, in a story. The events in the middle of the story are often attempts made to solve the main character's problem. Often, there are added difficulties for the main character. The events build to a **climax**, which is the turning point of the story. The climax, the point of the most powerful action, comes right before the end of the story, called the **resolution**.

Read the problem. Then, circle the paragraphs that might be part of the story's action.

1. **Problem:** Cheeser is supposed to play drums at the Mouse King's Ball, but he has to get past the cat first.

   a. Cheeser built a paper airplane to fly off the kitchen counter and over the cat. He was too heavy, and the plane crashed. Cheeser ran for cover!

   b. The next day, the Mouse King sent guards to arrest Cheeser.

   c. The dog outside began to bark when a car drove past the house.

   d. Cheeser practiced the drums for many years.

   e. The King once gave Cheeser a pair of cat whisker drumsticks.

   f. Cheeser hummed lullabies, trying to get the cat to fall asleep. The cat yawned but never slept.

   g. Cheeser shot some rubber bands at the cat, but the cat did not move.

   h. The cat had tried many times to catch the tricky mice. He only came close once, about three years ago.

   i. Cheeser flicked the kitchen lights to send a message to the Mouse King. The king sent soldiers as a decoy.

2. Choose the best climax for this story. Remember, the climax has the most powerful action.

   a. Cheeser gets caught by the cat, but the Mouse King's troops rescue him.

   b. Cheeser waits so long for the cat to fall asleep that he misses the whole ball.

   c. Cheeser runs past the cat but is too late to play the drums at the ball.

3. Write your own climax idea for this story.

   _____

   _____

   _____

                   IF87135 *Building Writing Skills*

Name _____

In the End

The **resolution** in the story is the ending. It is how the problem or conflict is solved. Sometimes the main character solves the problem. Sometimes the problem or conflict is resolved in other ways.

Read the problem statement. Then, decide if each following passage is part of the **plot** (an event) or the **resolution** (how the conflict is resolved). Write **plot** or **resolution** on the line.

1. **Problem:** Kenika's parents are getting a divorce. Her father wants her to live with him. Her mother also wants Kenika. They both want Kenika to make the decision.

    a. _____ Kenika asks both of her parents where they will live. Both choose to live in homes near her school. She would have her own room in either home. This information does not help her to decide.

    b. _____ Kenika explains to her mother and father that she would like to live with both of them. Since Mom travels during the week, she chooses to live with Dad at that time. She wants to live with Mom on the weekends when she is home. Her parents agree that Kenika made the best decision.

    c. _____ Her parents try to sway Kenika's decision by offering her video games and a pet. They each love Kenika and don't want to lose her.

Write your own plot and resolution to the following problem:

2. **Problem:** Your room is a mess. Your parents are always telling you to clean it up. You do not have enough space in your room for all of your things to fit neatly.

    Plot: _____

    _____

    _____

    Plot: _____

    _____

    Resolution: _____

    _____ _____

    _____

When the Chips Are Down

The way a story is organized is called the **story structure**. The setting, characters, and conflict are often set up in the beginning of the story. The plot, or series of events, continues through the middle of the story to a climax and the end. The conflict is usually resolved by the end of the story.

Read the story. Then, complete the story map on the next page.

It fell off again.

"It just won't work, Dexter," Sean said. "The pins are too loose on the chip."

"Maybe we could repair it. We sure can't afford a new chip like that," replied Sean's friend, Dexter.

Dexter's garage felt cool. The closed-in air held none of the summer heat that would later creep under the door or force itself through the thin glass of the only window. Still, there was only a week and a half before the science fair. The heat wouldn't matter at all after that.

Sean tried to reconnect the pin to the computer chip. The soft metal solder slipped into the space near the pin. After it cooled, Sean urged the pins into the motherboard.

"Oh, no! It broke again, Dex. This just isn't going to work," growled Sean.

"What do you think we should do now?" questioned Dex.

Sean simply shook his head. He knew that there was too little time to get enough money to buy the computer chip they needed to control the robot's "brain." Without that chip, it would be just like any other robot.

"Mom, would you be willing to lend Sean and me some money? We need it to finish our robot for the science fair," Dex said to his mother as she fixed dinner.

"You know I would help if I could, Honey, but we just don't have the money right now. I'll be happy if I'm able to pay the bills this month," his mother answered.

Dex called Sean to tell him the bad news. The boys decided to earn money in any way they could. Dex washed cars for some people on the block. Sean worked at his dad's shop cleaning up after the workers left at night. It was hard work, but he did it. Dex even babysat on Saturday night, which he really hated. If it meant money for the computer chip, though, he was willing.

They had only two days to go until the science fair. Dex and Sean slowly counted the money they worked so hard to earn. $62.30 was a lot of money, but not enough for the chip. They were $18.70 short. It was time to tell their science teacher, Mrs. Frommer.

"We tried, Mrs. Frommer, but we just can't get enough money for the chip to make our robot's brain," the boys told her sadly. "We tried hard."

Mrs. Frommer smiled. "I have just the thing!" she said. She opened her desk drawer and took out a slip of paper. The boys grinned when they saw it was a 25-percent-off coupon for the local computer store.

When the boys stood next to their exhibit, they had a robot that came to life.

story structure (cont.)   Name _____

◆◆◆◆◆◆◆◆◆◆◆◆◆◆◆◆◆◆◆◆◆◆◆◆◆◆◆◆◆◆◆◆◆◆

Complete the story map below by writing the setting, characters, problem, events, and solution for the story on page 62.

1. Setting   3. Main Characters' Problem

    when   _____   _____

    where   _____   _____

                                             _____

2. Characters   _____

        _____   _____

        _____   _____

        _____   _____

        _____   _____

◆◆◆◆◆◆◆◆◆◆◆◆◆◆◆◆◆◆◆◆◆◆◆◆◆◆◆◆◆◆◆◆◆◆

Events: What happens to keep the main characters from getting what they want? How is the main characters' problem resolved?

4. First,   6. Then,

    _____   _____

    _____   _____

    _____   _____

    _____   _____

    _____   _____

    _____

5. Next,   7. Finally,

    _____   _____

    _____   _____

    _____   _____

    _____   _____

    _____   _____

What's the Point?

The **theme** is the overall message or point of the book.

Below are some short summaries of stories. Possible **themes** are listed in the Theme Bank. On each line, write the letter of the theme that best matches each summary.

Theme Bank

a. Things aren't always what they seem.

b. Honesty is best.

c. Believe in yourself.

d. Deciding what's right isn't always easy.

e. Good is rewarded.

____1.   Once there was a girl who lived with her stepmother and stepsisters. The girl was kind, but she was treated unkindly. One day, her fairy godmother rewarded her by helping her go to a royal ball. There, she met a prince and fell in love.

____2.   Once Martin took a small apple from a fruit stand. He knew it was wrong, but he didn't have enough money, and he really wanted the apple. The next day, he went back and apologized to Mr. Wendell, the owner of the stand. Mr. Wendell was a kind man and understood. He gave Martin a job after school so he not only could pay for the apple, but also earn money for his family.

____3.   The mean old man glared at Sarah. All she did was say hello. She tried many times to be nice to Mr. Krupke, but he didn't seem to care. Her mother told her that Mr. Krupke's wife died many years ago. He was a sad man. Sarah asked if her family could have Mr. Krupke to supper. Thanks to new friends, Mr. Krupke smiled again.

____4.   The boys asked Jordan to join their basketball team. The only problem was that Jordan didn't know how to play. First, he told the others he was sick. The next time they asked him, Jordan said his family was going somewhere. He was embarrassed he couldn't play. Finally, he couldn't hide anymore. The others taught Jordan to play, and it turned out he was a great player. He had worried for no reason at all.

____5.   Devon looked around. He pulled a paper out of his desk with the spelling words on it. He carefully copied the word onto his test paper. I watched in disbelief. Devon quickly slid the other paper back in his desk as Mrs. Brenner passed by. I knew if I told Mrs. Brenner, Devon would get in trouble and be mad at me. But if I didn't tell, I'd be cheating, too.

Name _____

The New Kid

Narrative writing tells a story. Use a **story map** to plan a story.

Plan a story by making a story map from these ideas. Write the ideas into the plan where they fit best.

  a. First, Mr. Blanco introduced me to the other kids in the class.

  b. beginning of fifth grade

  c. Then, one brave boy said he'd show me around the school.

  d. Mr. Blanco, the class, and me

  e. Finally, other kids welcomed me to Boston and Freedom Trail Elementary.

  f. Freedom Trail Elementary School

  g. My family moved to Boston this summer. I'm the new kid here.

  h. Next, some of the kids teased me about my southern accent.

Story Map

  1. a. setting: _____

      b. characters: _____

      c. problem: _____

      _____

  2. first event: _____

      _____

  3. second event: _____

      _____

  4. third event: _____

      _____

  5. resolution: _____

      _____

You're the author! Write a story about the new kid using the story map above.

Whose Story Is It?

The **point of view** reveals who is telling the story.

first person: If a character tells the story, it is written in the first person.

Example: I rode as long as I could that day.

third person: A narrator is not a character in a story. The narrator speaks of "he" or "she" when describing characters.

Example: He rode as long as he could that day. By evening, he wondered why he was pushing so hard.

There are three third-person points of view:

- **omniscient:** The narrator can tell the thoughts and feelings of all the characters.

- **limited omniscient:** The narrator can tell the thoughts and feelings of only one character.

- **camera view:** The narrator cannot tell the thoughts and feelings of any characters. The narrator can only report what happens as events unfold.

Read each selection. Write **first-person**, **omniscient**, **limited omniscient**, or **camera view** to tell what point of view is being used in the sentence.

1. _____ The body of Abraham Lincoln slumped forward. There was a moment of startled silence. Everyone in the theater was shocked. Abbie Gale cried and crouched down in her seat. She shook with fear. Martin Lysen just stood and looked at the president. He could not believe what had happened.

2. _____ Ahmed stared out the window and cracked his knuckles. Omar kept shuffling a deck of cards and looking at the clock every few minutes. The small girl without a name dangled her legs off the table and slowly kicked the air. Shadows silently slipped across the floor.

3. _____ Theo quickly climbed the wall. As he slid down the other side, his hands ripped on the rough brick. He clenched his jaw tightly against the pain. He didn't want to let Les see that he was hurting. Les just ran ahead and waved for Theo to hurry.

4. _____ Mrs. Kluge pointed at me. Her finger waggled. I knew she'd seen me with the glowing rock. I wondered if she knew more, if she had touched it, too. That would explain why she had to turn her back on the class every fifteen minutes. She didn't want us to see.

◆◆◆◆◆◆◆◆◆◆◆◆◆◆◆◆◆◆◆◆◆◆◆◆◆◆◆◆◆◆

Rewrite this paragraph in the first-person point of view.

5. Willy held the bone so the dog could smell it. Then, he threw the bone far across the junkyard. The dog bolted after it. Willy hopped the fence and climbed onto the old shed. He looked for his mother's car.

_____

_____

_____

_____

_____

_____

Rewrite this paragraph in the camera-view third-person point of view. Remember, this narrator can tell what characters do, but not what they think or how they feel.

6. The two girls were so mad that they didn't speak to each other. Yolanda crossed her arms and leaned against the locker. She thought that Angel was mean. They both scowled. Angel clenched her fist and kicked the wall over and over. She was angry that she had to share a locker. She wanted her own locker.

_____

_____

_____

_____

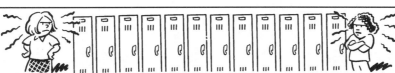

Rewrite this selection in the omniscient point of view. You will have to use your imagination to write about what the characters think or how they feel.

7. The walls of the cave wiggled in the candlelight. Dede and Ona huddled together. Dede whispered hopeful words to Ona. Ona shook. The water rose slowly.

_____

_____

_____

_____

_____

Name _____

Lead the Reader

A **hook** is the very beginning of a story. A good hook grips the reader and makes the reader ask questions. The reader wants to read the rest of the story to find out the answers. Here are three examples:

setting: The wind screamed, tossing aside trees and fences as it went.

character: Normally, old Widow Clacket would not leave the lamp burning.

action: She clung to the rope, hoping against hope that it wouldn't break.

Read each **hook**. Circle the letter of the question that it will most likely make the reader ask.

1. The night was too quiet and too dark. They should have heard some owls, a distant wolf, or at least the constant buzz of crickets.

    a. Who are *they*?

    b. Why was everything so quiet?

    c. Where was the moon?

2. Millie Louisa Post couldn't see over the crowd. She tried jumping, but everyone was too tall. Finally, she hiked up her dress and climbed onto a mailbox. She looked over the sea of people.

    a. What was the crowd there to see?

    b. How old was Millie Louisa Post?

    c. How tall was the mailbox?

3. Jela limped in from the fields when the sun was high. She only had twenty minutes for lunch. Mud caked her knees and hands. Dull, crusty lines showed where the sweat had dripped down her face. She leaned over the solid-gold washbasin and drowned her hands in cold water.

    a. Why were Jela's hands and knees dirty?

    b. How did a field worker get a solid-gold washbasin?

    c. Why was she limping?

4. From across the street, out a second-floor window, two cold eyes watched with interest.

    a. Was the street in a big city?

    b. What kind of building was across the street?

    c. Who was watching what?

Name _____

Secret Agents

Transitions help the reader follow a story. They show the order of events, a change in time or action, or how different ideas are connected.

Suddenly, Agent Bradski's escape route was gone.

Agent Xai sneaked into the compound **later that day**.

Early that morning, headquarters lost the radio signal.

Underline the transitions in these selections.

1. While Agent Jaquar climbed the outside wall, the final countdown started.

2. Agent Xai tried to reprogram the missile before the launch.

3. Earlier that day, enemy troops cornered Agent Bradski and captured her.

4. Meanwhile, the agents at headquarters finally unjammed the radio signals.

5. While on patrol duty, the guard saw the agent.

Write the transitions from the box into the sentences that follow.

a. before he programmed the missile.	c. With only one second on the timer,
b. After the mission was completed,	d. while Agent Xai was captured.

6. Agent Xai was captured _____

   _____

7. Agent Jaquar watched _____

   _____

8. _____

   _____ Agent Jaquar clipped the wires to stop the countdown.

9. _____

   _____ Agent Bradski radioed headquarters to tell of the successful mission.

Name _____

The Artist in Every Writer

Good writing allows the reader to see something in his or her mind. When writing, **don't tell** the reader what he or she should see; **show** the reader. Use words to paint a picture for the reader.

tell: The meadow was pretty.

show: The alpine meadow glistened with the early morning dew. Tiny white wildflowers bloomed in the meadow grass. The air was cool and fragrant.

Write **show** or **tell** in front of each sentence to explain how the writer used the words.

_____ 1. There was a storm. The ocean was rough. The water was blue and white.

_____ 2. The storm churned the blue ocean, tossing the waves high into the air. The waves foamed white as they returned to the arms of the waiting water.

In each oval, draw what you see when you read the text underneath the oval.

3. It was a nice day.   4. The sun shone brightly on the grassy fields where children flew colorful kites.

5. Which sentence paints a better picture? _____ Why? _____

_____

6. Rewrite this sentence to show, not tell: It was a hot day.

_____

_____

You're the author! Describe a place you like to go. Show, don't tell, with plenty of details.

Name _____

Let Your Feelings Show

Good writing allows the reader to see something in his or her mind. When writing, **don't tell** the reader what your characters feel; **show** the reader. Use words to paint a picture for the reader to see.

tell: Jasmine was sad.

show: Jasmine's head drooped as she walked down the hall. Tears filled her soft, brown eyes.

Read these telling sentences. Underline the words that tell how the character feels. Then rewrite the sentence to show how the character feels.

1. Yoon was afraid. _____
   _____

2. Mrs. Charlton is mad. _____
   _____

3. Fah Ali was very brave. _____
   _____

The following sentences show how various characters feel. Match each sentence to one of the feelings in the box.

a. tired	c. happy	e. sad
b. angry	d. excited	f. afraid

4. Mrs. Armstrong waved at every car that passed as she bounced down the sidewalk, humming a little tune. _____

5. Carlita slammed the pan onto the stove. She grabbed the meat and threw it onto the counter. It landed with a thud. _____

6. Gillie dabbed her eyes with the tissue. It didn't help. _____

7. Juan cartwheeled across the yard and jumped onto the fence, shouting and whooping. _____

8. Mr. De Bruyn's arms drooped by his side. His head tottered on his shoulders. He fell into bed. _____

Mabel's Magic Cakes

Action makes stories interesting to read. **Don't tell** the reader what happens in the story; **show** the reader. Help the reader feel he or she is there.

telling: Mabel felt very happy.

showing: Mabel danced across the room with a huge smile on her face.

Each selection has one sentence that **shows** instead of **tells**. Underline the showing sentence.

1.   Mabel baked a cake for some lucky person once a year on New Year's Eve. Everyone in the small town stood in the cold outside her house to find out who would get that year's cake. Excitement rattled through the frozen crowd like a pinball. The people could not wait to see Mabel's door open.

2.   Last year, Mabel baked a carrot cake for Deter Grabling, the old blind man. He cradled the cake in his arms and carefully shuffled toward home. He was so happy. The townspeople watched him go, telling each other how lucky he was.

3.   The townspeople went to see Deter the next day. He was excited. "I saw colors— bright as jewels, flashing and racing in front of my eyes. I've never seen colors before!" The crowd was thrilled. They loved Mabel's magic cakes.

These telling sentences do not paint a picture for the reader. Rewrite these sentences to show the reader.

4.   Deter talked to the crowd.

_____

_____

5.   The blind man saw colors.

_____

_____

6.   The people were happy for Deter.

_____

_____

show, don't tell (cont.)

◆◆◆◆◆◆◆◆◆◆◆◆◆◆◆◆◆◆◆◆◆◆◆◆◆◆◆◆◆◆◆◆◆◆◆

Read these paragraphs. Write a **showing** sentence in each blank. There is a hint under each blank to tell you what the sentence should describe.

This year, as usual, no one knew who would get the magic cake. Above Mabel's house, the moon shone as yellow and round as a cake itself. _____

1. The crowd talked while they waited.

_____

Suddenly, a warm, orange glow poured out of Mabel's door and onto the crowd. Mabel stepped into the light. She seemed to shine. She held up a cake for everyone to see. The townspeople hushed. _____

2. Mabel was happy as she walked through the crowd.

_____

Finally, Mabel stopped. She turned to look at a young orphan girl named Ellie. Both of Ellie's parents had died during the previous winter. The lonely girl now lived at the orphanage. She had not said a word to anyone for almost a year. Mabel knelt down in front of Ellie.

_____

3. Ellie was afraid.

_____

"You miss them, don't you, my dear?" asked Mabel.

Ellie nodded through her tears.

"I know, and I'm so sorry for you," said Mabel as she gave the girl a hug. "Maybe a nice angel cake would help you to feel better. Do you think it would?"

Ellie gave her a nervous smile and nodded again.

Mabel smiled and held out the cake. "Enjoy, my dear." She stood and walked back through the crowd. "Goodnight," Mabel said to her neighbors, smiling again. Then she seemed to just melt through the doorway and disappear.

The Nature of Nature

Quotation marks show a character's exact words.

- Put quotation marks outside of the punctuation that is included in the quote.

- Capitalize the first word of the quote, unless the quote is a partial sentence.

- Separate a quotation from the rest of the sentence with a comma, question mark, or exclamation point. Examples:

  "Nature tells every secret once," said Ralph Waldo Emerson.

  "Baa, baa, black sheep," the child sang, **"have you any wool?"**

  Henry David Thoreau wrote, **"The bluebird carries the sky on his back."**

If a quote is longer than one sentence, put the quotation marks at the beginning and after the end of the exact words or sentences that are said.

  No one knows who said, **"Nature is your fortune. Treasure it above all."**

Add the correct punctuation to these sentences.

1. All nature wears one universal grin stated Henry Fielding

2. Ralph Waldo Emerson said Nature and books belong to the eyes that see them

3. Everything has its beauty explains Confucius, but not everyone sees it

4. Albert Einstein said The most beautiful thing we can experience is the mysterious It is the source of all true art and science

Rewrite these quotes using correct punctuation and capitalization.

5. as Aristotle said nature does nothing uselessly

   _____

   _____

6. one touch of nature makes the whole world kin stated William Shakespeare

   _____

   _____

Name _____

Who Said What?

Dialogue is written conversation. When a different character speaks or when the main idea changes, begin a new paragraph. Remember, new paragraphs are indented.

indented: "They can't put a building there!" shouted Max. His arms were crossed, and he frowned.

indented: Zee scowled at the sign that said the empty lot had been sold.

indented: "What will happen to the fort?" asked Jalie. She looked over at their metal-sided hideout.

Read this dialogue. Put an X on each line where a new paragraph should begin. Leave the other lines blank.

1. The boys and girls crowded into the fort, a small shed with a metal roof and sides and two small windows. ___a. "Close the door, Zee," said Craft. ___b. Craft's real name was Paul, but no one ever called him that. ___c. Zee pulled the door closed and yanked the small lock into place. ___d. "Well," began Craft, "You all saw the sign. ___e. They sold our lot. That means they'll knock our fort down soon." ___f. "They can't do that," shouted Max. ___g. Max shouted often. ___h. "There's nothing we can do, Max," said Zee. ___i. Jalie sat quietly with a puzzled look on her face. ___j. Then she said in a soft voice, "Maybe, there is." ___k. Jalie was the thoughtful one in the group. ___l. She was good at solving problems. ___m. "What are you thinking, Jalie?" asked Craft.

This story selection should have many paragraphs. Rewrite it with the proper indentations.

2. "Look," said Jalie, pointing. "What?" shouted Max. "Hush, Max. Let her talk," said Zee. "Well, there's not really a floor, but the walls are connected to boards," said Jalie. "So we could drag the fort somewhere else," said Craft. "Great thinking, Jalie!"

_____

_____

_____

_____

_____

_____

_____

Name _____

Gauthier's Gator

Paragraphs help the reader understand when a new idea begins. Start a **new paragraph** whenever the **main idea changes** or **when a different character speaks**. Remember, new paragraphs are indented.

Rewrite this story, beginning a new paragraph when the main idea changes or when a different character speaks. Use another sheet of paper if necessary.

Bekah walked along the raised, gravel road. She was anxious to reach her friend's house. "Hi there, Mr. Gauthier," she called. "Hello, Bekah," he hollered back. Bekah liked Mr. Gauthier. He was always working in his yard. Mama said that he grew the prettiest flowers in seven states. "I am sure that's true," said Bekah softly to herself. As she rounded the corner, Bekah screamed. Peeking his snout out from under Lana's house was the biggest alligator Bekah had ever seen! She froze. She knew not to get close to a gator. Mr. Gauthier came running.

_____
_____
_____
_____
_____
_____
_____
_____
_____
_____
_____
_____
_____
_____
_____
_____
_____
_____

Name _____

End of the Day

At the end of a story, the **problem** or **conflict** is resolved. Sometimes the main character solves the problem. Sometimes the problem or conflict is resolved in other ways. The **climax**, the point of the most powerful action, comes right before the **resolution**.

Read the short story. Circle the letter of the ending that resolves the conflict.

1.   Ida Lee and Della stumbled toward the distant hills. They were tired and hungry, but even more, they were thirsty. The last water they had was the day before. The sun burned the two girls. They trudged on, moving toward the green hills and safety.

a.   The day got even hotter. The two girls found a huge boulder that gave them some shade. They rested until the sun moved toward the hills. Then they started walking again.

c.   The girls found a small grove of trees. They rested in the shade. Ida Lee dug under the tree. She cut some roots. The girls got a little water by chewing on the roots.

b.   The girls found a small grove of trees. Ida Lee dug up the roots. The girls chewed the roots to get a little water. They hiked throughout the night, exhausted, but were not able to reach the hills by morning.

d.   The two girls rested in the shade of a huge boulder. Ida Lee fell asleep. Suddenly Della heard a buzzing. It was a plane. She scrambled to the top of the boulder and waved at it, shouting. The girls were rescued.

2. Using your own ideas, write a different ending to this story. Remember that the conclusion must resolve the conflict.

_____

_____

_____

_____

_____

You're the author! Write about another problem the girls might have in the desert before they reach safety. How would this problem be solved?

What's in a Name?

The **title** is a very important part of a story. A title should give a clue about the topic of a story, but it should not give away the ending.

    example: *The Million-Dollar Movie*

The first word, the last word, and all important words in a title are capitalized. When book titles are printed in books or articles, they are in italics, *like this*. When you write a book title, underline it.

    In a book: *My Side of the Mountain*
    When you write it: <u>My Side of the Mountain</u>

Pick the best title for this story passage. Remember, a good title doesn't give too much away.

1.   The summit loomed just feet away. Sergio's feet ached from holding his weight on the tiny ledge that supported him. Suddenly, his brother's face appeared just above him. Nicoli lowered the rope to Sergio and pulled him to safety. Together, they conquered the wall of granite called El Capitan.

    a. *Conquering El Capitan*   c. *Challenging the Mountain*

    b. *Sergio and Nicoli*   d. *Safe Mountain Climbing*

Write a title for the story from which the passage below is taken.

2. _____

    The imposing, untamed horse strained against his tether. The rope weakened. As he reared and struck at the rope with his hooves, the rope surrendered and released him. Free and wild, the animal galloped across the sweet, brown earth with his nostrils flaring. He breathed in the scent of freedom.

Rewrite these book titles with the correct capitalization. Remember to underline each title.

3.   the call of the wild _____

4.   a wrinkle in time _____

5.   bridge to terabithia _____

6.   mrs. frisby and the rats of NIMH _____

_____

You're the author! Write a new title for your favorite book. Write a title for the history of your city or town. Write a new name for yourself. How did you decide what it would be?

Name _____

The Sum of the Parts

All of the words in the Word Bank are important parts of narrative writing. Use the clues to complete the crossword puzzle.

Word Bank

transitions
plot
hook
point of view
resolution
beginning
middle
end
dialogue
setting
climax
characters
title
conflict

Across

6. the last part of a story
7. shows who is telling the story
10. gets the reader's interest
11. highest point of action
12. events leading to a climax
13. how a story starts
14. people, animals, or things that do or say something in a story

Down

1. words used to show the order or relationship of events
2. the body of the story
3. the name of the story
4. how the problem is solved
5. the problem or difficulty
8. where and when the story takes place
9. characters talking in a story

Check it out! Enjoy your favorite book. As you read, find all of the story parts. For example, what is the conflict? How is it resolved? What is the climax?

Name _____

Whoosh!

Onomatopoeia is the use of words that sound like their meanings. Using these words makes writing more interesting.

The machine **clicked** and **whirred**, but it still didn't work.

My mother's favorite dish fell to the floor with a **crash**!

Read these sentences. Write the words that are examples of onomatopoeia on the lines.

1. The wind whooshed through the trees.

    _____

2. When the woods were quiet, we heard a twig snap.

    _____

3. The windows rattled as the earthquake shook the cottage.

    _____

Underline any words in this selection that sound like their meanings.

4.   The swamp behind Lane Roy's house is filled with sound. Toads and tree frogs croak in the evenings. Sometimes the chirping of the crickets is so loud that you can't hear the little frogs. But the booming *bree-deep* of the big bullfrogs can always be heard. Each bird has its own sound, too. There are loud caws, soft whistles, and cheery trills. Even the buzz of mosquitoes has its place in the swamp. I don't know how Lane Roy sleeps with all that racket going on!

    croak   peep   peep   peep   peep   peep   peep   peep   peep   peep

5. Write a paragraph about a trip. Include six words that show onomatopoeia.

    _____

    _____

    _____

    _____

    _____

    _____

    _____

Jovial Jobs

- **Consonance** is a consonant sound repeated anywhere in a series of words.
  A **d**entist **d**rille**d** **D**a**d**'s tooth.
- **Alliteration** is a beginning consonant sound repeated in a series of words.
  Policeman **P**eters **p**atrolled the corner of **P**atterson and **P**iedmont.
- **Assonance** is a vowel sound repeated anywhere in a series of words. Remember that vowels and combinations of vowels can make more than one sound.
  A v**e**t will h**e**lp your p**e**t's h**ea**d g**e**t b**e**tter.

You can use consonance, alliteration, and assonance to create "special effects" in your writing.

Read each sentence. Tell whether the author uses consonance, alliteration, or assonance by writing the word on the line before each sentence. Also, write the letter sound or sounds that are repeated.

1. _____ Five firefighters fought the flaming house.

2. _____ Doctor Waddle delivered a baby boy.

3. _____ Snake tamers stay away from the fangs.

4. _____ Mr. Reilly really wanted to ride in a rodeo.

5. _____ The eye doctor sighed when I couldn't find the chart.

6. _____ Two telephone operators sat down to visit.

Read this paragraph. Find examples of consonance, alliteration, and assonance. Write all the words from the example on the lines. Remember to listen for a sound, not look for a letter.

My dad is a tractor salesman. He travels from town to town, talking with farmers. He can't bring his tractors with him, so he shows the whole set of tractors with photos. Dad loves telling the farmers about his tractors. He gathers them all together and tells them what there is to know. My dad is very good at his job.

7. example of consonance: _____

8. example of alliteration: _____

9. example of assonance: _____

You're the author! Write your own sentences using consonance, alliteration, and assonance.

Name _____

Smart as a Whip

A **simile** compares two things using the words **like** or **as**. In writing, comparing things can make your meaning clearer.

Major Garcia had a voice **like** a cannon.

My sister is as gentle **as** a lamb.

Velma was as white **as** a ghost.

Write the words from the Word Bank on the blanks to complete these similes.

Word Bank	
rock	swan
drums	fish

1. Her long, graceful neck made her as beautiful as a _____.

2. The thunder boomed like distant_____.

3. Dahlia won the swim meet because she swims like a _____.

4. Jimmy Trueheart's promise is as solid as a _____.

Write your own similes to describe these things.

5. Dad remembers that huge turtle from when he was a boy.

    That turtle is as big as _____.

6. I carried the boat across the rocks. It wasn't too heavy.

    The boat is as light as _____.

7. When the principal spoke, everyone could hear him.

    The principal is as loud as _____.

8. After coming in from playing in the snow, Kayli's nose was frozen.

    Her nose was as cold as _____.

You're the author! Write three similes to describe your favorite animal.

Name _____

She Is an Angel

A **metaphor** compares two things without using the words **like** or **as**. Using metaphors in your writing helps to emphasize your point.

He is a mule. I can't get him to change his mind.

That mountain is a monster. No one has ever been able to climb it.

Read each metaphor. Then circle the letter that tells what the metaphor means.

1. Alphonse is a workhorse.

   a. Alphonse is big.

   b. Alphonse smells like hay.

   c. Alphonse works hard.

2. Chelle is an angel.

   a. Chelle is not real.

   b. Chelle is kind.

   c. Chelle has wings and a halo.

3. I was a tiger on the prowl.

   a. I was growling with anger.

   b. I was wearing my striped pajamas.

   c. I was very quiet and stealthy.

4. Mr. Macgregor is a dinosaur.

   a. Mr. Macgregor has rough skin.

   b. Mr. Macgregor likes dinosaurs.

   c. Mr. Macgregor is out of touch with new ideas.

5. That test was a bear.

   a. The test was about types of bears.

   b. The test was very hard.

   c. My stomach was growling during the test.

Write your own metaphors to describe these:

6. a tree that is taller than all the others

   _____

   _____

7. a man who works very slowly

   _____

   _____

◆◆◆

Like a Dream

A **simile** compares two things using the word **like** or **as**.

> **He was as stubborn as a mule.** I couldn't get him to change his mind.

A metaphor compares two things without using the word **like** or **as**.

> **He is a mule.** I couldn't get him to change his mind.

Comparing things can make your meaning clearer and emphasize your point.

◆◆◆

Write an **S** for simile or an **M** for metaphor to tell what type of comparison is made in each sentence. Then, write down what the simile or metaphor might mean.

_____ 1. Mr. Murray is a packrat. _____

_____ 2. Uta is as sweet as pie. _____

_____ 3. Shel sometimes rages like a storm. _____

_____ 4. That guy is a weasel. _____

_____ 5. The thief was as slippery as an eel. _____

_____ 6. You are a dream. _____

_____ 7. The sunset is a painter's palette. _____

_____ 8. Kirby is like a junkyard dog. _____

_____ 9. I slept like a baby. _____

_____ 10. Mary is a bookworm. _____

Name _____

I Could Eat a Horse

A **hyperbole** is an extreme exaggeration. Use a hyperbole to emphasize your point.

example: I am so hungry that I could eat a horse!

Write an **H** if the sentence is a hyperbole. Otherwise, leave the line blank.

_____ 1. That shop serves mile-high ice cream cones.

_____ 2. That box weighs a ton.

_____ 3. Hercules was very strong.

_____ 4. That hole is so deep it goes straight through to China.

_____ 5. Michael Johnson can run faster than anyone I know.

_____ 6. I jumped so high that I hit my head on the moon.

_____ 7. We scared Mrs. Bradley to death.

Write your own hyperboles, or exaggerations, for these sentences. Remember to write in complete sentences.

8. I was thirsty. _____

_____

9. Cabe was tired. _____

_____

10. Georgiana's sandwich was big. _____

_____

11. Kimberly's room was dirty. _____

_____

12. I was late. _____

_____

Check it out! Read a tall tale. How many hyperboles can you find? Write your own tall tale. Remember to use hyperboles.

◆◆◆◆◆◆◆◆◆◆◆◆◆◆◆◆◆◆◆◆◆◆◆◆◆◆◆◆◆◆◆◆◆◆◆◆◆◆

Autumn Is Alive

Personification means giving **human qualities** to animals or objects.
example: The leaves **skipped** and **danced** down the sidewalk.

◆◆◆◆◆◆◆◆◆◆◆◆◆◆◆◆◆◆◆◆◆◆◆◆◆◆◆◆◆◆◆◆◆◆◆◆◆◆

Underline all the examples of personification in these paragraphs.

1.   Every October, autumn bullies summer into letting go of the skies. The wind breathes a chill into the air. The sun gets tired and goes to bed earlier each night. The trees dress in bright gowns for the last celebration of the season. Soon, the leaves are skipping and dancing down the sidewalk, and the trees stretch their empty hands up to the moon. Morning sometimes drags a blanket of frost over the grass. Night sleeps in later each day. This is autumn, standing firm with hands on her hips, until winter peers over the edge of the world.

2.   Each autumn, the leaves are invited to a costume party. They wear their finest colors. The young leaves sometimes forget to change from their green clothes. The older leaves wear the faded, brown suits they've worn too long. They all gather together to chatter and dance. Arm in arm they swing and swirl, twist and twirl. Some dance quickly in small circles, others waltz slowly across the ground. They prattle on about falling from the arms of the trees. Then, when only a few leaves are still able to dance, winter arrives and plays a different song.

Write your own ideas about how to personify each item. Remember, to personify means to give human qualities to objects or animals.

3.   the moon   _____

4.   birds   _____

5.   air   _____

6.   winter   _____

7.   sky   _____

8.   animals   _____

You're the author! Write a paragraph about a storm. Use personification.

Name _____

What Next?

Foreshadowing is hinting or offering clues to the reader about what will happen in the story.

example: Nothing unusual ever happens at Rockpoint Middle School, or so we thought. (This hints that something unusual will happen.)

If each paragraph selection hints about something that might happen, write **foreshadowing** and then tell what you think might happen. If there is no foreshadowing, leave the lines blank.

1.   Stinky Blevens started bragging to everyone as soon as his brother stepped up to the plate. "My brother always hits a homerun," taunted Stinky. Boy, was he in for a surprise.

   _____

   _____

   _____

2.   The explorers gathered on the dock, checked in, and walked up the gangplank to the *Chance*. Emelio told the doctor he felt well. Actually, he felt a little sick to his stomach, but at the time, he thought it was nothing to worry about.

   _____

   _____

   _____

3.   Tessa was the smartest girl in the school. She didn't need to study, but she always did. That's why her test score was so earthshattering.

   _____

   _____

   _____

You're the author! Write a story beginning that hints about what might happen. See if your friends can guess what is going to happen next in your story.

Name _____

The GTS Timebender

Foreshadowing is hinting or offering clues to the reader about what will happen in the story.

Normally, a Golorian Time Ship is very reliable. (The word "normally" hints that something might go wrong with the ship.)

Some of the sentence ideas foreshadow the events at the bottom of the page. Select the letter of the sentence that foreshadows each event below and write it on the line.

a. Never look a Tchi-Yant in the eyes; it is considered an insult.

b. A GTS can only be tracked if its time drive is not running.

c. Captain Radu always makes sure his ships have escape pods—just in case.

d. Tchi-Yants are dishonest, but they trade the most valuable goods.

e. A GTS can fly at TS-80, twice as fast as a tracking sensor can operate.

f. Normally, a Golorian Time Ship, or GTS, is very reliable.

g. All GTSs have a time drive for distances, and a harmonic drive for local travel.

Events

_____ 1. Captain Radu finally found someone who had a Golorian Time Ship. Radu was led to a back room and told to sit down. The creature on the other side of the desk grinned wickedly and rubbed its many hands together. It was a Tchi-Yant, of course.

_____ 2. The whine and clatter from the time drive told Captain Radu what he did not want to know. Their ship, the GTS *Timebender*, was in trouble. *But this kind of problem never happens!* thought Radu.

_____ 3. "We are being tracked," reported the computer.
Captain Radu looked up from the damaged time drive. "What took them so long?" he said. "Engage shields and warm up the harmonic drive!"

_____ 4. A loud crash and a distant explosion was all that Captain Radu could hear through the thick walls of the escape pod. A quick burst of speed pulled him away from what was left of the GTS *Timebender*. He was glad he talked the Tchi-Yant into including the pod in their deal.

Name _____

Science Fair

Tone is the writer's attitude about the subject or topic. The writer's tone can be funny, serious, sarcastic, persuasive, etc.

Match each sentence to the tone that the words create.

_____ 1. sad   a. That's why we should all work hard to conserve energy.

_____ 2. happy   b. I never win things like this!

_____ 3. funny   c. There is nothing funny about pollution.

_____ 4. serious   d. I can't believe I won first place!

_____ 5. technical   e. After I glued part A onto part B, I inserted the cotter pin.

_____ 6. persuasive   f. The first time I tried this, I ended up with spaghetti in my hair!

Circle the letter of the word that describes the tone of each paragraph.

7.   I never quite know what to do when teachers say we are having a science fair. First, they say we need to pick a topic. The good experiments like exploding volcanoes and solar-powered cars were all done last year. So what's left? Then, they make us do research. That means a trip to the library filling out those index cards, which always get lost or mixed up. Couldn't we just use notebook paper? Then there's the display. Playing football is easy, but writing in marker on a poster board is the worst. I hate science fairs!

a. humorous   b. serious   c. persuasive   d. frustrated   e. happy

8.   The point of this study was to figure out how much energy a normal household uses. First, I did a survey of the homes marked with red lines on the map. The four questions on the survey are listed on the chart. Residents of the homes gave the answers. Then, I used the infrared pictures to find out which homes were losing heat through the roof. These homes are marked in yellow on the map. Finally, I compared the heat lost with the energy used. With these numbers, it was easy to find an average. Also, these numbers help to predict how much energy a home might use, based on the size of the home and the infrared pictures.

a. humorous   b. serious   c. persuasive   d. frustrated   e. happy

Get an Attitude!

Tone is the writer's attitude about the subject or topic. The writer's tone can be funny, serious, sad, persuasive, etc.

Rewrite this sentence using the different tones listed.

Today, I got a C on my math test.

1. (happy)   _____

2. (frustrated) _____

3. (technical) _____

Choose a concluding sentence to match the tone of the paragraph.

4.   I just know there are aliens somewhere in the universe, and I have proof. First of all, there have been UFO and spaceship sightings all around the world. A lot of the sightings could be fake, but I prefer to believe they are real. Secondly, our dog E.T. barks at the moon all the time. Is he trying to communicate with someone out there? I think he is! The last reason I think there are aliens out in space is that my brother has been speaking some strange language lately. Dad says he's taking German, but it doesn't sound like any language *I've* ever heard before.

   a. Could my weird brother be living proof of life from other planets?

   b. I feel, in conclusion, that no proof of alien life leaves the question open-ended.

5.   Of all of the fantasy books I have read, *The Hobbit* by J. R. R. Tolkien is the one I will never forget. There are many places in his book, like Mirkwood and Smaug's lair, that I will never forget either. The way Tolkien wrote about them, I could picture the places in my mind and be right there along with his characters. Gandalf is an old wizard who is very wise. Bilbo, the hobbit, finds a magic ring that makes him invisible. The best part of this story is the characters. They all seem like people I have met; however, no one could meet the hobbit, the dragon, or the wizard because Tolkien's mind created them. They don't really exist. Or do they?

   a. In fact, Tolkien gave us the gift of his imagined world for all time; that's why I love reading and why I love this book.

   b. The fact is that magic is not real; now that I'm older, I feel cheated by this book.

Name _____

A Toolbox

Literary devices are **tools or techniques** a writer uses when writing a story.

Each clue below is an example of a tool or technique a writer might use. Read the clues. Then, complete the crossword puzzle using the literary devices in the Word Bank.

Across

2. I'm so hungry that I could eat a horse!

7. She was a gentle breeze.

9. omniscient or first person

11. This would not be the last time.

12. Five fine frogs fished for fun.

Down

1. The little tattletales wanted toys.

3. He was seen with a green machine.

4. The tick-tock of the clock kept him awake.

5. She was like a gentle breeze.

6. The wind cried.

8. She heard the eerie sound again that night.

10. humorous, serious, sad, jubilant

Word Bank

simile	hook
foreshadowing	hyberbole
point of view	personification
metaphor	consonance
onomatopoeia	alliteration
tone	assonance

Name _____

The Northern Lights

When choosing a topic, it is important to know the **purpose** for writing. The writer must also know who the readers, or audience, will be.

Match the topic to the correct purpose and audience. Write the letters and Roman numerals on the lines.

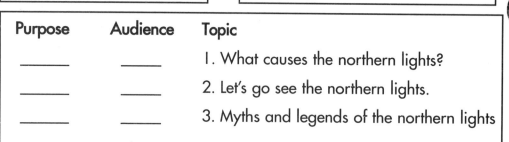

Purpose	Audience
a. share information	I. parents
b. entertain	II. science fair judges
c. persuade	III. classmates and teachers

Purpose	Audience	Topic
_____	_____	1. What causes the northern lights?
_____	_____	2. Let's go see the northern lights.
_____	_____	3. Myths and legends of the northern lights

This paragraph was written for a specific purpose and audience. The purpose was to give information about the northern lights. The audience was a class and its teacher.

The northern lights are a beautiful display of science at work. They are caused by the solar wind, a stream of particles from the sun. The particles hit the upper atmosphere and begin to glow. Vivid colors, from reds and oranges to blues and greens, seem to fall out of the sky. The colors flow like curtains in a breeze. People can view the northern lights at night in Alaska and other northern lands. The lights used to be seen as omens or spirits. They are still viewed with awe. Science is incredibly beautiful!

Rewrite the paragraph above to persuade your parents to take you to see the northern lights.

_____

_____

_____

_____

_____

Name _____

Aurora Borealis

A **prompt** is an idea or starting point for writing. Sometimes a writer must write to a prompt. It is important to know what is being asked and what type of writing is required.

Expository writing gives information or explains something.

Persuasive writing tries to talk someone into something.

Narrative writing tells a story.

Write **expository**, **persuasive**, or **narrative** on the line to tell what type of writing is required for each prompt.

1. _____ Write a paper to explain the different colors in the aurora.

2. _____ Imagine the first people to see the northern lights. What might they think they were seeing? What would they feel? Write about their possible thoughts and feelings.

3. _____ Write a letter to your teacher, asking for his/her permission to research the northern lights for the science fair.

4. _____ Write a note to convince your parents to take you to see the northern lights.

5. _____ Write a report about the name *aurora borealis*.

6. _____ Write a story about how the northern lights once helped someone who was lost in the wilderness.

Imagine you are the leader of a northern tribe. Write a brief tale to tell your tribe what the lights are and what they mean.

_____

_____

_____

_____

_____

_____

_____

A Most Unusual Light

Staying on topic means making sure the reader follows the writer's ideas. If the writer includes information that is about the topic, the reader could become confused.

topic:	the northern lights
on topic:	The northern lights can be seen at night in the far north.
off topic:	My cousin took a picture of some lights in the sky.

Read each report. Cross out the sentences or paragraphs that are not **on topic**.

Omens of the Northern Lights

Many Native American tribes believed that the northern lights, or aurora borealis, were an omen. An omen is a sign of something to come. An omen can predict something good or bad. The holy people of the tribes would decide what the omen of the northern lights meant.

Tribes in the mountains and river valleys of South America never saw the northern lights. They had different omens, based on the weather. A drought, a time with little water, meant that the gods were not happy.

Different tribes believed the lights meant different things. Some Native Americans believed the lights were an omen of war. Others thought the lights were the spirits of humans or animals wandering in the sky. Still others believed the lights were torches used by spirits who were in heaven. The Fox and Sauk tribes saw the northern lights, too.

The lights were very important to all these tribes. They might prepare for war or have a celebration when they saw the lights. The lights brought happiness, sorrow, or fear. Therefore, in some ways, the northern lights really were omens of things to come.

Solar-Powered Light Show

The aurora borealis is truly a solar-powered light show. The sun emits charged particles in all directions. A cloud of these particles is called *plasma*. The stream of plasma coming from the sun is called the solar wind. The wind on earth is made up of air molecules.

When the solar wind hits the earth, some of the charged particles get caught. They move along the earth's magnetic lines at the north pole. When these particles hit the gasses in the earth's atmosphere, they glow. The light that comes from these glowing particles is called an aurora.

Since the aurora is electrical, it can cause problems with radios and satellites.

Different types of air molecules make up the different colors. Oxygen makes a greenish-white color. Nitrogen makes the reddish colors. Other colors come from other air molecules.

These beautiful colors and lights are visible at night in the northern skies. The aurora borealis is nature's magnificent light show, powered by the sun.

Name _____

More Details, Please

After writing, go back to **revise**, or make your writing better. One way to do this is to **elaborate** by adding details. Details could include examples, explanations, or descriptions.

before revising: Strange colors glowed in the sky.

after revising: Wisps of green, blue, and red glowed in the black sky.

Read each sentence. The hint tells what kind of detail to add to the sentence. Circle the letter of the revised sentence that adds that type of detail.

1. The northern lights are beautiful. (add description)

   a. The northern lights are dazzling curtains of red, blue, and green.

   b. The northern lights are a result of charged particles from the sun.

   c. The northern lights are often seen in Canada and Alaska.

2. The northern lights are made of glowing particles. (explain)

   a. The northern lights are curtains of red, blue, and green from the air.

   b. The northern lights result from charged particles from the sun hitting our air.

   c. The northern lights are most often seen in the upper atmosphere.

3. The colors come from different air molecules. (give examples)

   a. The colors are dazzling reds, blues, and greens from air molecules.

   b. The different colors come from air molecules like oxygen, which makes green.

   c. Nitrogen makes one of the colors of the aurora.

Read each sentence. Then, revise it to add the type of detail given in the hint.

4. The northern lights are colorful. (add description)

   _____

   _____

5. The northern lights can be seen in the north. (give examples)

   _____

   _____

Nature's Splendor

Specific words tell the reader more than vague or unclear words.

vague sentence:	The lights were in the sky.
vivid verbs:	The lights **danced** in the sky.
vague sentence:	The lights floated above the planet.
names:	**The aurora borealis** floated above the **earth**.
vague sentence:	He saw colors in the sky.
specific words:	He saw **red**, **green**, and **blue** in the **night** sky.

Select the sentence that is the most specific to describe these topics.

1. Topic: the lights of the aurora

   a. The lights of the aurora shine in the night sky of Canada and Alaska.

   b. The fantastic lights of the aurora shine beautifully.

   c. The lights of aurora borealis shimmer with green, blue, and red colors.

2. Topic: lights are seen in lands in the north

   a. The lights can be seen in Canada, Alaska, northern Europe, and Siberia.

   b. The fantastic lights of the aurora shine beautifully in the northern skies.

   c. Greens, reds, and blues dance mysteriously in the northern lights.

3. Topic: how the aurora looks

   a. The lights of the aurora shine in the sky.

   b. The lights of the aurora look like waves of colors fanning across the sky.

   c. The lights of the aurora attract the attention of every person who sees them.

4. Topic: the aurora is a sight that should not be missed

   a. Go see the lights of the aurora if you can.

   b. Everyone should have the chance to see the northern lights.

   c. A journey to a northern region to see the aurora borealis is well worth the trip.

You're the author! Write a paragraph to persuade someone to go see the aurora borealis.

Name _____

Carlos's Wagon Wheel

Each pronoun in a sentence takes the place of a specific noun. If the reader cannot tell which noun goes with the pronoun, the sentence can be confusing. These sentences need to be **revised**.

confusing:	Carlos rode Snuff, his black donkey, until he was tired. (Who was tired, Carlos or Snuff?)
revised:	Carlos rode Snuff, his black donkey, until Carlos was tired.
confusing:	Carlos was hauling books and medicines to the town because they were desperately needed. (What was needed—books, medicines, or both?)
revised:	Carlos was hauling books and medicines to the town. The medicines were desperately needed.

Read each sentence. Write down the noun or nouns that go with each pronoun. If the meaning is unclear, revise the sentence at the bottom of the page.

1. Carlos watched the wagon and the wagon wheel closely because he was afraid it would break.

   What noun goes with <u>it</u>? _____

   What noun goes with <u>he</u>? _____

2. The wheel started wobbling and then it snapped.

   What noun goes with <u>it</u>? _____

3. Carlos looked for a spare wheel and a hammer, but he could not find one.

   What noun goes with <u>one</u>? _____

4. Carlos sawed off the top of a tree trunk and put a hole in the middle of it.

   What noun goes with <u>it</u>? _____

Rewrite the unclear sentences here.

5. _____

   _____

6. _____

   _____

Name _____

Too Slow and Steady

When a writer uses the same kind of sentence over and over, the reader can get bored. Changing the length and type of sentence can make a piece of writing more fun to read. Make your writing better by **revising** for:

- complete sentences,
- a variety of sentence length, and
- a variety of sentence structure—simple, compound, and complex.

Rewrite these sentences correctly.

1. The tortoise is slow, the tortoise is steady.

   _____

2. Are endangered. People harm the tortoises' habitats.

   _____

Rewrite this report. Vary the sentences and make any fragments into complete sentences.

3.   Giant tortoises live on the Galapagos Islands. They have thick shells. They have hard, scaly legs. Have hinged shells. The hinged shell can close. Use the shell to hide from predators. No animals can hurt them—except human beings. People brought goats to the islands. The goats eat too much grass. The tortoises do not have enough to eat. Someone needs to help the giant tortoises. They are endangered.

_____

_____

_____

_____

_____

_____

_____

_____

_____

_____

Name _____

Siva, from Bombay

Editing means checking the writing to find errors.

• Errors can be found with the subject—noun or pronoun.

• The pronoun form may be incorrect—me or I, he or him, she or her.

• The subject may repeat when it should not—Mrs. Smith, she is nice.

• Errors can be found with the verb.

• The verb may not agree with the subject.

• The verb may be in the wrong tense—past, present, or future.

• The verb may not be spelled correctly.

These sentences all have errors. Rewrite the sentences correctly.

1. Siva, he is from India, a country in Asia.

_____

2. He comed from a city called Bombay.

_____

3. Next year, Siva will went to high school.

_____

This paragraph has several subject errors and verb errors. Cross out all the words that are incorrect. Write the corrected words above them. The first one is done for you.

Siva came to the United States last year to study. He ~~leaved~~ left

his family back in India. When he come to America, he told his

family that he would miss them. Siva, he writes a letter to they

every week. He tells them about his studies, his friends, and his

life in the United States. Siva wants to be a teacher in India.

After he studies for four years here, he went home to his family.

He sayed he cannot wait to see them again. His family cannot

wait, either. They miss he.

99   IF87135 *Building Writing Skills*

◆◆◆◆◆◆◆◆◆◆◆◆◆◆◆◆◆◆◆◆◆◆◆◆◆◆◆◆◆◆◆◆◆

Gum–Everlasting

Editing means checking your writing to find errors. One type of error is incorrect spelling.

◆◆◆◆◆◆◆◆◆◆◆◆◆◆◆◆◆◆◆◆◆◆◆◆◆◆◆◆◆◆◆◆◆

The person who wrote these advertisements did not check for spelling errors. Read each ad. Cross out the misspelled words and write the corrected words above them.

Gum–Everlasting

Does your gum lose its flavor?

Dose it gets hard after only twelve hours?

You need too try new Gum-Everlasting.

WHY?

Yule get all-day chewing enjoyment!

You'll also get our new, high-tech Gum Reflaviator. Put you're old gum inside the Reflaviator befor you go to bed. When you get up in the morning, your gum is sotf, flavorful, and ready for another day. So, bye your Gum-Everlasting today!

Brother Be-Gone

Chessa had a big problem—her brothers. When she goed to her room to play with her friends, her brothers allways followed them. Thay teased Chessa and laught at her.

Chessa tryed Brother Be-Gone. She sprayed Brother Be-Gon around her room. That was the end of her problem! Chessas brotters stood by the door, but they could'nt came into her room.

Do you hafe a brother?
You need Brother Be-Gone!

You're the author! Write an ad for a brand-new toy. Edit your ad for spelling, punctuation, capitalization, and complete sentences.

         IF87135 *Building Writing Skills*

Love, Grandpa

Editing means checking the writing to find errors.

• Check for proper **capitalization**. The editing mark for capitalization looks like three underlines: a̲ Some of the items that need capitalization are:

- the beginning of sentences.
- proper nouns.
- titles of books and movies.
- sentences that start inside quotation marks.

• Check for correct **punctuation**. Punctuate:

- the end of sentences.
- commas in dates, addresses, and series.
- commas in compound and complex sentences.
- quotations.

Help Grandpa Joe correct his errors in capitalization and punctuation before he sends this letter to his great-grandson, Randy. Make three small lines under each letter that should be capitalized. Add any needed punctuation.

123 memory lane
El Monte CA 92403
january 12 2001

Dear Randy,

    I had a great time at your house! I sure enjoyed the meal you and your mom made for me. the hamburgers potato salad and homemade pie were all perfect Thank you very much!

    I also want to thank you and your mom for the hand-knit sweater. The neighbors saw me wearing it on a walk. esther said "that's the prettiest sweater I've ever seen" I told her that my great-grandson gave it to me. You are such a thoughtful boy!

    The very best part of our visit was sharing songs with you. I love to play the guitar. I am glad you love it, too Let's get together to play and sing some more. maybe I can even learn some of that electric guitar music that you play.

Love,
Grandpa Joe

Name _____

Break it Up

The editing mark to show where a new paragraph should begin looks like this: ¶. Begin a paragraph whenever there is a new main idea or whenever a different character speaks. Remember that transition words, such as **first**, **then**, **often**, can help you find where a new idea begins.

This story was written as one paragraph. Use the paragraph symbol to show where the author should have started new paragraphs.

The race judges had to pull the two boys away from each other. ____a. The first boy, Petre, was tall and thin with wild, fuzzy, blond hair. ____b. His face and ears were red. ____c. Petre had won the downhill cart race the last two years. ____d. The other boy, Sig, was from town. ____e. He was small and dirty from head to toe. ____f. His shocking blue eyes were the brightest part about him. ____g. Sig's father was the laughing-stock of the town because he always tried to invent crazy things. ____h. "Now, what's this all about, boys?" ____i. asked one of the race judges. ____ j. He looked at Petre and said, "It's not like you to fight, Petre." ____k. Petre spoke quickly and in a harsh voice said, "He started it. ____l. He tried to break my cart before the race!" ____m. "I did not!" shouted Sig. ____n. The two boys started yelling again. ____o. "Quiet!" shouted the judge. "Now, you first, Petre. Just tell me what happened—nothing more," he added in a soothing voice. ____p. Petre said quickly, "I left my cart for a few minutes. When I came back, Sig was under my cart and his hands were doing something I couldn't see." ____q. "I see," said the judge. "And what about you, young man? What happened?" asked the judge. ____r. At the judge's urging, Sig finally said in a soft, choppy voice, "My pa's working on a new thing. It's got wheels. He tried to move it, but it wouldn't go where he wanted. ____s. When I saw Petre's cart, I wanted to see how he made the cart turn. I looked at his because, well, because his cart is the best." ____t. Sig looked at the ground. He bit his lip. ____u. The judge smiled. ____v. "There you go, Petre," he said, "the boy was just looking because your cart is the best."

____w. "I guess, um…I'm sorry I jumped on you," said Petre, his ears even redder. ____x. "I'm sorry I didn't ask before I looked," said Sig. ____y. The two gave each other a small smile.

You're the author! Write a story about a race. Remember to start a new paragraph whenever there is a new main idea or when a different character speaks.

           IF87135 *Building Writing Skills*

Short but Sweet

Short answers should be written in complete sentences. They need to be supported with at least two details from the reading or text. Remember to use the question words in the answer.

question: What makes a good short answer?

poor answer: complete sentence with information

good answer: A good short answer is a complete sentence supported with at least two details from the text.

Read the selection and the question. Circle the best short answer. Remember that a short answer is a complete sentence with at least two details from the text.

The honeybee is a very valuable insect. It does much more than make honey. The most important role of the honeybee is to pollinate plants. The bee doesn't intend to do this. A honeybee collects pollen and nectar from a flower. When the bee goes to the next flower, some of the pollen from the first flower falls onto the second flower. The second flower uses this pollen to make seeds. The seeds grow into more plants. Scientists have guessed that honeybees help pollinate $10 billion worth of crops a year in the United States. This is why the honeybee is so important.

1. Why is the honeybee an important insect?

   a. Because it pollinates plants and makes honey.

   b. The honeybee is an important insect because it carries pollen from plant to plant and makes seeds for new plants.

   c. The honeybee is an important insect because it collects pollen and nectar from plants, and uses these to make honey.

   d. It is important because it pollinates plants.

   e. The honeybee is an important insect because it pollinates plants, helping to support about $10 billion worth of crops a year.

2. How does the honeybee pollinate plants?

   a. The honeybee pollinates plants as it flies from flower to flower to gather pollen and nectar; this causes the pollen to mix.

   b. The honeybee is important because it pollinates plants. When it gathers pollen, it helps support about $10 billion worth of crops.

   c. Flies from flower to flower and mixes different pollens.

   d. By carrying pollen from one flower to another and making seeds.

   e. The honeybee pollinates plants when it makes honey and seeds.

Get the Message

A **summary** is a short version of the original written work. A **one-sentence summary** tells the title and author as well as the theme. The **theme** is the overall message or point of the book.

Examples:

A Wrinkle in Time by Madeleine L'Engle reveals that with love, anything is possible.

Hatchet by Gary Paulsen illustrates the strength of the will to survive.

Read the selection. Answer the questions.

Mulanko by Philip Mark

Mulanko was raised in Nigeria, Africa. His father was a marathon runner. Mulanko wanted to run a marathon with his father, but the boy could not run far enough. A marathon is a little more than forty-two kilometers. Mulanko could only run twenty.

"The key," said Mulanko's father, "is to believe in yourself. The human body can really only run about sixteen kilometers. So if you want to run more than forty, you have to do it in your head, by believing you can. If you can run twenty kilometers, you can run forty-two. There's no difference."

Mulanko knew he could run twenty kilometers. If his father was right, then he could run forty-two. He trained for another long run. This time, Mulanko ran the full marathon. His father was very proud. But no one was prouder than Mulanko.

1. Circle the letter that indicates the best **one-sentence summary** of the selection.

   a. *Mulanko* by Philip Mark shows that anyone can run forty-two kilometers.

   b. *Mulanko* shows that fathers and sons understand each other.

   c. *Mulanko* by Philip Mark shows that you can do anything if you believe in yourself.

   d. *Mulanko* by Philip Mark shows the best way to train for a marathon.

2. Circle the letter that indicates the **theme** of the selection.

   a. If you can run twenty kilometers, you can run forty-two.

   b. Running a marathon is the best way to get your father's approval.

   c. You can do anything if you believe in yourself.

   d. Fathers and sons should share the same hobbies.

Name _____

Butterfly Girl

To summarize narrative writing, or stories, you can use information from a story map or outline that you make while you read. The **summary** should include some story elements, such as setting, characters, conflict, plot, and resolution.

Read the short story. Then choose the best summary. Remember that the summary should include some of the basic story elements.

Gabriella, a shy and lonely student, played the part of a sad caterpillar in her school play in the second grade. At the end of the play, she broke out of a paper cocoon and spread her wings to become a happy butterfly. That was four years ago. Something in the play made sense to Gabriella. She started to think about how sad things could change and become happy.

In third grade, Gabriella started drawing butterflies. "That's beautiful work," said her teacher. "You have a talent for art." Gabriella started smiling a little more often.

In fourth grade, Gabriella stopped staring at the ground at recess. Instead, she tried talking to some of the other students. Kareena became her friend. Gabriella smiled even more that year.

In fifth grade, Gabriella started playing soccer. She found she could be an important member of a team. In fact, her teammates voted her "Most Valuable Player" at the end of the season. Gabriella smiled a lot.

Today in class, Gabriella watched a caterpillar. It was slowly climbing up a twig, maybe on its way to make a cocoon. The shiny, black back of the caterpillar rolled in tiny waves as it moved. A shimmer of green and blue moved along its back when the light was just right. Gabriella suddenly realized that the small creature was beautiful. She hoped it wouldn't make its cocoon just yet. She wanted to watch it grow a little bigger.

a. In the fourth grade, Gabriella watches a caterpillar become a butterfly. She thinks back on how she learned how to play soccer and became an artist.

b. Gabriella learns about how caterpillars become beautiful butterflies when she is in the second grade. Gradually she discovers her talents and becomes happier and more confident. When she feels better about herself, she discovers that even caterpillars can be beautiful.

c. Gabriella starts out being shy, but then she starts drawing butterflies. She smiles more. One day, she sees a beautiful caterpillar.

d. Gabriella learns how to make friends and play soccer. She thinks of herself as a caterpillar, but she draws butterflies instead.

◆◆◆◆◆◆◆◆◆◆◆◆◆◆◆◆◆◆◆◆◆◆◆◆◆◆◆◆◆◆◆◆◆◆◆

Not My Words

Paraphrasing is restating something in different words. To check for understanding while reading, stop reading and write about what you read in your own words.

◆◆◆◆◆◆◆◆◆◆◆◆◆◆◆◆◆◆◆◆◆◆◆◆◆◆◆◆◆◆◆◆◆◆◆

Read each selection. Circle the letter of the sentence that best paraphrases the selection.

1.   I believe the great Native American chiefs knew more than most people about the natural world. They knew there was a balance in nature, that the bad events were offset by good events. In addition, they knew that they had to take care of the land. I wish more people knew what the great chiefs knew.

    a. The author believes the great chiefs knew more than most people about the natural world. He thinks they knew there was a balance in nature and that they had to take care of the land. The author wishes more people knew what the great chiefs knew.

    b. The author believes Native American chiefs knew a lot about nature and balance. He wishes more people knew about taking good care of the environment.

    c. The author knows more than most people about the natural world. He knows about natural balance, and that people have to take care of the world.

2.   Abraham Lincoln had to be careful before the Civil War. He did not want the Union, the northern states, to start the war. He may have felt that if the Union started the war, more people would support the Confederacy, the southern states. When the Confederacy fired on Fort Sumter, many people supported Lincoln and the Union. It may be true that the Union won the war, in part, because it did not start the war.

    a. The author believes that since Lincoln did not start the Civil War, more people supported the Union, or northern states. This may have helped the North to win.

    b. Abraham Lincoln had to be very careful before the Civil War. He felt that if the Union started the war, more people would support the southern states. It could be true that the Union won the war, in part, because it did not start the war.

    c. The author feels that President Lincoln was smart before the war. He believes that if the Union had started the war, they would have been able to win. Since the Confederacy started the war, more people supported the South.

Name _____

Primary Colors

Taking notes helps people think about and remember information that they read. Taking notes means to write down only the most important information from a passage, or reading. The first step in taking notes is finding the main idea.

Read each paragraph. Take notes on another piece of paper to help you summarize the ideas in each paragraph. Then circle the letter of the sentence that best presents the main idea.

1.   How many colors are there? When you set up a new computer monitor, you can choose color settings like sixteen colors, 256 colors, or "true color." Does that mean there are only 256 true colors? It is easy to imagine there are millions of shades of colors. How many of those different shades are true colors? You may be surprised to learn that there are only three.

   a. There are many shades of colors, but only three true colors.

   b. Computers have different color settings.

   c. There are millions of shades of colors.

2.   Every color is made by combining primary colors. There are two different sets of primary colors. The primary colors of *pigments* are red, blue, and yellow. Pigments are found in paints, dyes, and inks. However, the primary colors of *light* are red, blue, and green. Light makes colors when refracted through a prism or seen on a video monitor. By mixing different amounts of primary colors, you can create all the other colors.

   a. There are colors of light that you can't even imagine.

   b. Green, purple, brown, and all the other colors are called created colors.

   c. There are two sets of primary colors, one for light and one for pigments, each of which can be mixed to make new colors.

3.   So how are colors mixed? By mixing different amounts of the primary colors, whether it's with paints or on your computer screen, millions of colors and shades can be created. If you only mix red and blue, you see purple. The exact shade of purple depends on how much red and how much blue are mixed together.

   a. Every color comes from mixing some combination of primary colors together.

   b. All colors are created from primary colors, and the different amounts of each color create the different shades.

   c. Mixing red and blue light on your computer screen makes purple.

A Few Notes on Dogs

Taking notes means to write down just the most important information. The first step in taking notes is finding the main idea. Then, write down the most important details.

Read this report. Then, use the Idea Bank to create notes for the two paragraphs that follow the introduction in the report.

Did people in the Middle Ages have pet dogs? Did the ancient Romans keep dogs? Dogs and humans have lived side-by-side for a long time, but does anyone really know when this relationship began?

Scientists believe dogs first learned to live with humans over 14,000 years ago. A cemetery for dogs was found in an ancient Persian empire in the Middle East. The cemetery dates to the fifth century BC. More proof exists in a statue that looks like a dog, found in King Tutankhamen's tomb in Egypt. The statue has been dated 1,400 BC. Fossil records and artifacts show that dogs were workmates and playmates to humans long before the statue or the cemetery. But why?

No one knows exactly how, why, or when dogs and people started living together. There were many advantages for both dogs and humans. Dogs were used to help people hunt, herd, guard, attack, alert, and rescue. Dogs could destroy rats, pull sleds, and carry messages. The dogs, in return, received food, shelter, love, and attention. Perhaps dogs were the ones who chose to live with humans. If so, that may have been the luckiest day in human history.

second paragraph

1. main idea _____
   _____
2. detail _____
   _____
3. detail _____
   _____

third paragraph

4. main idea _____
   _____
5. detail _____
   _____
6. detail _____
   _____

Idea Bank

a. very old fossils and artifacts show dogs

b. maybe dogs chose humans

c. dogs have lived with people a long time

d. dogs got food, shelter, and love

e. a dog cemetery in Persia

f. living together good for humans and dogs

g. scientists say more than 14,000 years

h. a dog statue

i. dogs can hunt, herd, guard, and rescue

j. no one knows how, why, or when

Giants of the Desert

An outline is a plan for a piece of writing. It contains the topics or ideas about which you will write. The ideas are written from general to specific. Often, the ideas are written in words or phrases, not complete sentences.

The outline may be broken into as many sections as needed, but no topic may have just one supporting idea listed under it.

Outline

I. Plan for writing

   A. contains topics

      1. general to specific

      2. not in complete sentences

   B. is in sections

      1. as many as needed

      2. no idea with just one supporting statement

The outline on the right was the plan for this article. Read the article and replace the missing information in the outline.

The Saguaro Cactus

The saguaro (suh-WAH-r) are majestic cacti that grow to be fifty feet (15m) tall and weigh nine metric tons. The saguaro, however, grows slowly. It may only grow a few feet in fifty years, but it can live for two centuries!

These remarkable cacti live in one of the hottest and driest parts of North America. In the summer, the Sonoran Desert is often over 100 degrees (38 C). In the winter, the temperatures are mild, but with only ten inches (254mm) of rainfall a year, the desert is very dry.

Luckily, the saguaro, like other cacti, have adapted well to their environment. They flourish in the desert, and drink the precious water when it is available. The sharp spines that cover their stems keep animals from eating them. Their lovely white, waxy flowers are the state flower of Arizona. These giant beauties reign supreme over their home in the hot, dry, Sonoran Desert.

Outline for The Saguaro Cactus

I. Giant of the Sonoran Desert

   A. size

      1. fifty feet tall

      2. _____

   B. lifetime

      1. grows slowly

      2. _____

II. Habitat—hot and dry

   A. 100° summers, mild winters

   B. _____

III. Special Features

   A. drinks when water is available

   B. sharp spines keep animals from eating them

   C. _____

   D. conclusion

◆◆

Whose Fault Is It?

An **essay question** requires more than a short answer. Like a prompt, an essay question offers clues about what type of answer is required.

- Read the question two or three times to be certain you know what is being asked. Look for clue words like **compare, contrast, definition, discuss, explain, describe, cause and effect**, and so on.
- Brainstorm main ideas and details for answering the question.

◆◆

Read the essay. Answer the questions.

The earth is covered with a thin layer of rock called the *crust*. It is similar to the crust on the top of a pie. The layer of rocks floats on top of a layer of molten rock. The crust is made up of many plates, or masses, of rock. When heat from the inside of the earth creates stress in the crust, the crust breaks. The place where the crust breaks is called a fault.

Many times, the earth's plates move along an existing fault. Often, faults can be seen in areas where a hill or mountain has been cut for a road. Some faults are even visible from the air, especially if they are major faults, such as the San Andreas Fault in California. When the plates of rock move suddenly along a fault, the result is an earthquake.

Read each question at least twice. Circle the letter for the type of paragraph you would write to answer each essay question.

1. What causes a fault?

    a. how-to

    b. cause/effect

    c. compare/contrast

    d. problem/solution

2. How would you describe the earth's crust?

    a. cause/effect

    b. problem/solution

    c. explanation

    d. description

3. If you were going to answer question 2 above, which ideas would be appropriate to use in your answer? Circle all that apply.

    a. thin layer of rock

    b. the San Andreas is an example of an existing fault

    c. floats on top of molten rock

    d. made up of plates

    e. has faults, or areas where the earth has broken

    f. earthquakes are caused by faults

    g. plates are not stable, they move

    h. hills or mountains should be cut to find faults

                       IF87135 *Building Writing Skills*

Name _____

It's Not My Fault

An **essay question** requires more than a short answer. An answer to an essay question is expository writing; it explains or gives information. It must be supported with facts or opinions. First, determine what the question is asking and brainstorm ideas. Then, follow these steps:

- organize the ideas into a plan for writing
- turn the question into a topic sentence
- write the answer clearly, with supporting facts or opinions

Organize your ideas from question 3 on page 110 into a writing plan.

main idea: _____

detail: _____

detail: _____

main idea: _____

detail: _____

detail: _____

Read the following essay questions. Write each question as a topic sentence by adding whatever information you need from your plan. Answer the last essay question completely.

1. What causes a fault to form in the earth's crust?

    _____

2. How would you describe the earth's crust?

    _____

3. How would you describe the earth's crust? Use your topic sentences and writing plan to answer.

    _____

    _____

    _____

    _____

    _____

Walking a Thin Line

A **summary** is a short version of the original written work. To write a summary, find the main ideas. Then, find the important details. From this information, write a summary.

Underline the topic sentences in each of these paragraphs. Underline the most important detail from each paragraph.

Do you know the name Charles Blondin? Have you ever heard of Niagara Falls? Charles Blondin is famous for his amazing performances at Niagara Falls.

Charles Blondin was a tightrope walker and acrobat. He was born in Saint-Omer, France. His real name was Jean François Gravelet. He became known as the Little Wonder for his daring performances when he was only six years old.

This French acrobat is most famous for his performances over Niagara Falls, which began in 1859. He stretched a rope 1,100 feet (336 m) from one side of the falls to the other. The rope was 160 feet (49 m) above the falls. To the amazement of the crowd, Charles Blondin crossed the falls on the thin rope. How could anyone top such an incredible feat?

Charles Blondin topped his own performance at least four different times. He later crossed the Niagara Falls blindfolded, and then he pushed a wheelbarrow across the tightrope. During another crossing, he carried a small stove and other equipment. He stopped halfway across to cook and eat an omelet! The Little Wonder of France became a big name around the world.

1. Choose the best summary based on the topic sentences and important details.

   a. Charles Blondin, or Jean François Gravelet, topped his own performances at least four different times. He crossed blindfolded, with a wheelbarrow, and with a cooking stove. Charles became the most famous tightrope walker in the world. He was called the Little Wonder.

   b. Charles Blondin was a tightrope walker. He began performing when he was only six years old. He was known as the Little Wonder, but his real name was Jean François Gravelet. He was born in France.

   c. Charles Blondin was a French acrobat and tightrope walker. He was known as the Little Wonder when he began performing at the age of six. His most famous performances began in 1859, when he crossed the Niagara Falls on a tightrope. He crossed at least four more times, making each crossing more dangerous than the one before.

Name

Neuschwanstein

A **summary** is a short version of the original written work. Newspaper articles are written with the most important information first. Use the same techniques newspapers use when writing a summary. Include **who** or **what**, **(did) what**, **where**, **when**, and **why** in your summary.

In this article, underline the sentences that tell **who** or **what**, **did what**, **where**, **when**, and **why**.

Neuschwanstein is the name of a famous castle in Germany. The name means "New Swan Castle," and it was built by King Ludwig II of Bavaria. King Ludwig II had built and remodeled many castles before this one. Neuschwanstein was to be his dream castle. However, it took so long to build that Ludwig did not live to see it finished.

Construction on the castle began in 1869 and lasted seventeen years, until the king's death in 1886. Work stopped when the king died. In 1890, a small piece of the castle was completed, but no other work has been done. The second floor and other parts of the castle are completely unfinished.

Even unfinished, Neuschwanstein is stunningly beautiful. Grand mountains surround the castle. Many blue-tipped towers reach up to the sky. A strong gate stands across the arched entry. The castle is perched on the top of a mountain. The whole scene seems magical. In fact, Walt Disney used Neuschwanstein as the inspiration and model for Sleeping Beauty's Castle in Disneyland.

Eventually, the king's extravagance caused him to lose his throne. Even his own doctor once said that the king was insane. However, no one can deny that his dream castle, Neuschwanstein, is one of the most beautiful in the world.

1. Circle the best summary that includes who or what, did what, where, when, and why.

   a. Although King Ludwig II of Bavaria was thought to be insane, he built many splendid castles. The king died in 1886, before his dream castle, Neuschwanstein, was completed.

   b. Neuschwanstein, a castle in Germany, was built by King Ludwig II of Bavaria. The main construction of the castle halted when the king died. Although King Ludwig's dream castle was never finished, it is thought to be one of the most beautiful castles in the world.

   c. Neuschwanstein was designed as the dream castle of King Ludwig II of Bavaria. He had it built from 1869 until 1886. Construction stopped because the king died. Neuschwanstein is considered to be one of the most beautiful castles in the world.

An Egyptian Thank-you

A **letter** has five parts: a **heading**, a **greeting**, a **body**, a **closing**, and a **signature**. Each part has its own place in a letter.

The **greeting** and **closing** should begin with a capital letter. Other words that are not names use lowercase letters. A comma follows both the greeting and the closing.

examples: My dear best friend, (greeting) or With my love, (closing)

This letter was not written in letter form, and there are some other errors. Rewrite this letter correctly by writing each part in its proper place. Correct the mistakes as you fill in the blanks.

a. Lee Bahney

b. October 18 2002

c. Very Truly Yours

d. On behalf of my class, I would like to thank you for your talk about Egypt's history and culture. Everyone enjoyed the pictures and artifacts you shared. We really learned a lot.

e. Hayes elementary school
    20500 Kings Blvd.
    Athens, GA 07209

f. dear Mrs. Bradley

1. _____

   _____

   _____

   heading

2. _____

   date

3. _____,

   greeting

4. _____

   _____

   _____

   _____

   _____

   _____

   _____

   _____

   body of letter

5. _____

   closing

6. _____

   signature

Name _____

Signed, Sealed, and Delivered

Addressing an envelope is the last step before sending a letter. Two addresses appear on an envelope. The **mailing address** goes in the front center of the envelope. It tells who will receive the letter. The **return address** goes in the upper-left corner of the front of the envelope. It shows who is sending the letter.

An address includes a name, a number and street name, a city, a state, and a zip code. All words should be capitalized. A comma separates the city and state.

> Mr. Avery Schimke
> 1234 Silver Springs Drive
> Bangor, Maine 00432

Rewrite the following address correctly.

1. nadine may hayward _____

   298 rose lane _____

   jackson mississippi 36946 _____

What is missing from each of the following addresses?

2. _____

   Mr. Edward Hughes

   Eucalyptus Street

   Riverside, California 92507

3. _____

   Mrs. Ralph Valjean

   1489 Kessler Blvd.

   Indianapolis 46299

4. Write your own name and address for the return address. Correct and use the following address for the mailing address:

   mrs helen colles, 845 pine street, garnet montana 55608.

Name _____

Pebble Rings, Like Memories

Poetry tells about feelings, ideas, or events, often with fewer words than regular writing. Some poems rhyme and some poems do not. A poem can be whatever the writer wants it to be. Poems may not always have complete sentences, but they are often capitalized at the beginning of each line.

Poems take many forms. Some are written in stanzas, or groups of lines. Some play with language including sounds, meanings, similes, metaphors, and personification. Often, poems have rhythm.

Read the poem and answer the questions.

Pebble Rings, Like Memories

The old stone bridge across Rügen Bay
Is one of my favorite places to play.
I toss pebbles for Mom, and a pebble for Dad,
And a rock for the horses and the chickens we had.
I watch as each of the stones makes rings
Like the songs that each of my memories sings.
For my wife—for my dear and precious Lenore—
My hands and my eyes throw several more.
And then, before my playing is done
I throw the most important one,
For the memory of my son.

1. Write down one example of a simile from the poem. _____

2. Write down two examples of rhyming words. _____

3. How old does the author seem after the first three lines? _____

4. How old does the author seem at the end of the poem? _____

5. Is the author happy or sad? How do you know? _____

_____

You're the author! Write two more lines that could be added to this poem.

Name _____

Couplets and Quatrains

A **couplet** is a pair of rhyming lines. They can be combined into longer poems, like the **quatrain**, which is made up of two couplets. The **a** lines rhyme with other **a** lines, and **b** lines rhyme with other **b** lines. Normally the lines are around the same length and tell about the same subject.

Sometimes the rhymes are together like this:		Sometimes the rhymes are apart like this:	
Carrots, beans, or peas?	a	A timeless tree stood	a
Who wants to eat these?	a	on the edge of a dream,	b
I won't tell a lie.	b	and thought that he could	a
We want to eat pie!	b	run like the stream	b

Read each line of poetry. Write a line of poetry from the Idea Bank to make a couplet.

1. The wolf tried so hard to get to sleep,

    _____

2. To breakfast, to school, to dinner, and then

    _____

Make up your own lines to complete this couplet.

3. If you want bad luck, then get a black cat

    _____

Make up your own lines to complete this quatrain using the **aabb** pattern.

4. At the end of the day, when the sun climbs down
    And the bashful moon wears a silvery gown,

    _____

    _____

> ### Idea Bank
> a. He ate sheep.
>
> b. Great big bugs began to creep.
>
> c. But lost his count when he ate the sheep.
>
> d. Cows in the barn and pigs in the pen.
>
> e. Get up the next morning and do it again!
>
> f. to bed.

You're the author! Write a quatrain about something you enjoy.

       IF87135 *Building Writing Skills*

Name _____

Cleri—Who?

A **clerihew** is a fun, sometimes humorous poem. It is made up of two couplets in the rhyming pattern **aabb**. It is about a famous person or celebrity. The first line ends with the person's name.

example: He never told a lie, George Washington,
                  except for maybe for a little one.
                  His dad found the chopped-down cherry tree
                  and Washington said, "It wasn't me!"

Two clerihews were scrambled together. Unscramble them and write them on the lines.

a. but would rather sleep than car-chase!

b. When Old Mother Goose

c. with ears long, black, and droopy

d. but then came a crack and a yelp.

e. One famous dog named Snoopy

f. had a tooth that was loose,

g. Humpty Dumpty said he'd help

h. would fight a World War I ace,

1. _____

   _____

   _____

   _____

2. _____

   _____

   _____

   _____

Write your own clerihew about someone famous or someone you know.

_____

_____

_____

_____

Name _____

Electric Etheree

An **etheree** is a ten-line poem with a specific number of syllables per line. The first line has one syllable, the second line has two syllables, and so on, up to the tenth line with ten syllables. An etheree does not rhyme and tells about only one idea.

Count the number of syllables in each line of the Idea Bank. Write the numbers on the lines.

Idea Bank

a. a zero-watt bulb _____

b. I shine like a light at night _____

c. magnetic glow _____

d. Am I a nightlight? Am I a boy? _____

e. And I have _____

f. But a twenty-watt me _____

Write lines of the poem from the Idea Bank in the blanks where they belong in this etheree.

Zap!

A shock,

1. _____

2. _____

A zero-watt bulb,

But a twenty-watt me.

3. _____

and I can't seem to fall asleep.

4. _____

Now I am a glow-in-the-dark brother.

5. What do you think happened to make the boy glow? _____

_____

_____

6. What clue does the "zero-watt bulb" give you about what happened? _____

_____

_____

Answer Key

◆◆◆◆◆◆◆◆◆◆◆◆◆◆◆◆◆◆◆◆◆◆◆◆◆◆

1. sentence
2. fragment
3. sentence
4. sentence
5. fragment
6. sentence

Answers 7 and 8: A very old city. Because running with the bulls can be dangerous. Rewritten sentences will vary.

1. imperative/yellow
2. declarative/purple
3. exclamatory/blue
4. interrogative/red
5. declarative/purple
6. interrogative/red
7. imperative/yellow

1. Twenty thousand ant species live on our planet.
2. Some species can sting their prey.
3. Most ants live for less than six months.
4. Queen ants can live for several years.
5. Ant nests are often found underground or beneath logs.

6. d
7. e
8. b
9. a
10. c
Additional sentences will vary.

1. Humans and mice can solve mazes.
2. Mice and humans like to eat cheese.
3. Humans are able to reason and speak. or, Humans are able to reason and are able to speak.
4. Mice eat and sleep in their nests.
5. Humans and mice care for their babies.
6. Mice wake up and look for food at night. or, Mice wake up at night and look for food.

1. One exciting event
2. It
3. One of the most graceful winter events
4. The U. S. Women's Hockey Team
5. Bonnie Blair
6. She
7. 1998 Winter Games; Winter Games; or Games
8. Picabo Street
9. He
10. It
11. Answers will vary.

1. wished
2. slipped
3. hoped   a. sailing
4. cried   b. guided
5. splashing   c. applied
6. clapping   d. trimmed
7. waking   e. worked
8. replying

1. am
2. is
3. Are
4. are
5. are
6. was
7. were
8. were
9. was
10. was

1. sat
2. do
3. spoke
4. wished
5. have
6. hummed
7. felt
8. are
9. were
10. stepped
11. ran
12. saw
13. heard
14. is
15. asked
16. did or do
17. pulled
18. left

1. simple
2. compound
3. simple
4. compound
5. simple
6. compound
7. A few men found gold, and other men came to find gold. or, to find some gold.
8. Gold is what brought the men to the towns, but the gold soon ran out. or, The gold soon ran out, but the men still wanted to be rich.

1. Samuel Clemens was twenty-five when he and his brother moved to Nevada.

Answer Key

◆◆◆◆◆◆◆◆◆◆◆◆◆◆◆◆◆◆◆◆◆◆◆◆◆◆◆◆◆◆◆◆◆◆◆◆◆◆

2. They lived in Carson City, because Sam's brother worked there for the Territory office.
3. Because he wanted to see the silver mines, Sam traveled to Aurora in 1861.
4. When he returned to Carson City, Sam published articles in a newspaper.
5. b.
6. While he worked as a writer in Virginia City, Nevada, Samuel Clemens first used the pen name Mark Twain.

The Fourth of July! (sentence variety) 14
1. (I) like the Fourth of July.
2. (The red, white, and blue colors) are so pretty in all of the decorations.
3. (My family and I) like to go to the parade to see the floats and hear the bands.
4. (The music) is so patriotic!
5. Even though (we) like the music (we) also like the barbecue after the parade.
6. (We) always have to wait our turn when we get to the food stand.
7. (I) like the hamburgers best, although (my brother) likes the hot dogs.
8. After we get our food, (we) find a nice, shady spot to eat.
9. (The first song) is happy, but (the second song) sounds sad.
10. (It) reminds Dad of his Army friends, and (Mom) puts her arm around him.
11. (The time for the fireworks) is here, and (I) can hardly wait!
12. (We) see flashes of blue and yellow, but (we) hear thunderous booms.
13. (Dad) drives us home, and (we) dream about next year.

Autumn Leaves (sentence variety) 15
1. S
2. S
3. C
4. CX
5. S
6. CX
7. S
8. S
9. C
10. CX
11. S
12. CX
13. C
14. S
15. CX

Railroad to the West (combining sentences) 16
1. Railroad owners wanted more tracks, and President Lincoln gave them land.
2. Many men worked on the railroad to the West, and the tracks were finished in 1869.
3. The first railroad to the West was done, and other tracks were later laid to the West.
4. Men built the railroad to the West while the Civil War was fought.
5. Many new settlers moved west after the tracks were finished.
6. Although building the railroad was very hard, the new tracks helped America.

Answers 4, 5, and 6 may vary slightly.

Malik the Magician (run-on sentences) 17
1. The magician waved his wand. The girl floated in the air.
2. The boy picked a card. Malik already knew which card.
3. Malik popped the balloon. A dove flew out of the balloon.
4. A girl pulled Malik's scarf, and a flower popped out of his pocket.
5. Malik opened the box, but the boy was not inside.
6. The magician dropped the rope into a bag, and a snake slithered out of it.

Go Fly a Kite (stringy sentences) 18
1. Caleb's kite is caught in the tree. He climbs the tree. He gets the kite down.
2. The biggest kite belongs to Janelle. She doesn't know how to fly it very well. Her father helps her.
3. Chung flies a yellow kite, and everyone can see it on a cloudy day. It is cloudy today.
4. I like to fly my kite, but there is not enough wind right now. I'll try tomorrow.

Sentences 3 and 4 may vary slightly.

The Mighty Eagle (correcting sentences) 19
1. run-on; Female eagles stay near the nest. Male eagles hunt for food.
2. stringy; Eagles swoop from the sky. Some eagles pluck fish from the water, but they fly to a safe place to eat.
3. stringy; Golden eagles nest on cliffs. The nest is hard to reach. The eagles can protect their chicks.
4. run-on; The bald eagle is the national bird of America, but the bald eagle is not really bald. or, The bald eagle is not really bald.
Sentences may vary slightly.

Dear Detective (comma review) 20
Paris, France
October 6, 2001
September 23, 2001
We searched the museum, but the ring could not be found. I put my keys on a table, and they were gone five minutes later.
While we were in a meeting, the rock was taken from her desk.
October 3, 2001
We do not know what kind of thief would take keys, rings, and rocks.

Answer Key

◆◆◆◆◆◆◆◆◆◆◆◆◆◆◆◆◆◆◆◆◆◆◆◆◆◆◆◆◆◆◆◆

The Missing Items (description) 21
  1. a. valuable; b. three; sparkles; e. velvet
  2. a. silver; b. parrot; c. carefully; d. soft
  3. a. broken; b. smooth; c. third

Bigger and Brighter (comparisons) 22
  a. older
  b. oldest
  c. largest
  d. bigger
  e. brightest
  f. smaller
  g. smallest
  h. bigger

Where Were You? (elaboration) 23
  1. c
  2. b
  3. b
  4. Answers will vary.
  5. Answers will vary.

Why Did It Happen? (elaboration).................24
  1. b
  2. d
  3. a
  4. c
  5. g
  6. h
  7. e
  8. f

Great Scott! (elaboration) 25
  1. when
  2. how
  3. where
  4. how

The Main Goal (paragraphs) 26
  1. e
  2. b
  3. f

The Windy City (extraneous details) 27
  1. a; People in cities choose school boards too.
  2. b; Fires cause a lot of damage every year.
  3. b, d

Horses at Work (topic sentences) 28
  1. b
  2. a
  3. Answers will vary

Yeeeehaw! (topic sentences) 29
  1. Rodeos began long ago when cowboys wanted to see
     who was the best at roping and riding.
  2. There are many events in a rodeo.
  3. One of the most exciting events in a rodeo is the bull
     riding.

Lead Me to Egypt (leads) 30
  1.   For 4,500 years, the Great Pyramid of Khufu at
       Giza was the tallest building in the entire world.
  2.   Did you know that ancient Egypt influenced the
       United States dollar bill?

Tornado! (supporting sentences)....................31
  1. a, c, f
  2. c, d, f
  3. a, d, f

Brrrrrrrr! Bears! (examples) 32
  1. Their black skin absorbs heat, and their hollow hairs
     shield their bodies from the cold.
  2. They have their wide feet and stiff hairs on their legs to
     push against the water.
  3. Polar bears cover their black noses with their paws
     while they hunt.

Flying Byrd (transitions) 33
  1. First, Next, Another, Then, Finally
  2. a. First, ; b. Then, ; c. Third, ; d. One, ; e. Finally,

Steps to the New World (sequencing) 34
  1. First,
  2. Second,
  3. Next,
  4. Then, (Next and then are interchangeable.)
  5. Finally,

Land! Land! (concluding sentences) 35
  1. a
  2. b
  3. Answers will vary.

Let Me Explain (concluding sentences) 36
  1. b
  2. b
  3. a

Computers and Homework (expository paragraphs) 37
1, 3, 4 for supporting sentences.
  a. 1
  b. 3
  d. 4

My Brother's Shoes (expository planning) 38
  1. e
  2a. g
  2b. c
  3a. i
  3b. a
  4a. b
  4b. h
  5. j

Komodo Dragons (paragraphing/indentation) 39
  Paragraphs to indent: a, c, e

Answer Key

◆◆◆◆◆◆◆◆◆◆◆◆◆◆◆◆◆◆◆◆◆◆◆◆◆◆◆◆◆◆◆◆◆◆◆

The Iditarod (paragraphing/indentation) 40
Indented sentences:
The Iditarod Trail Sled Dog Race began in 1973.
In the early 1900s, the town of Iditarod was a gold rush town, halfway between Anchorage and Nome.
Today, the Iditarod Trail is used for sport: man and dogs against the environment.

Introducing the Incas (informative paragraph) 41
Cross out: b, d, g, i, j
Paragraphs will vary; however, sentences that have not been crossed out should all be used. Topic sentence: a
Concluding sentence: c or h

The Incas and Us (compare and contrast) 42
Circled sentences: 1, 2, 3, 4, 6, 9
Venn: Incas: a, d, e
both: f, g, i
North Americans: b, c, h

Picture This (descriptive) 43
1. huge, snow-capped/sight
2. small, brown, grass-roofed, adobe/sight
3. cold blast/touch
4. rumbling bray/sound
5. bitter-corn/smell
6. spicy/taste
7. heavy, woolen, rough as stiff, dry grass/touch
8. distant cries/sound

Problems for the Incas (problem/solution) 44
1. a or d
2. Answers will vary.

Next Stop, Machu Picchu (how-to) 45
1. plane tickets to Lima and from Lima to Cusco
2. train ticket to the trailhead in Chilca
3. backpack
4. camping supplies

map: draw a line from point of origin to Lima and from Lima to Cusco; draw a line along the train tracks from Cusco to Chilca (Abacay); follow the trail to Machu Picchu.

Let's Go! (persuasive) 46
1. against
2. for
3. against
4. against
5. for
6. against
7. for
8. for
9. for
Paragraphs will vary; should include three "for" reasons.

The End of the Incas (cause and effect) 47
1. b
2. e

3. a
4. c
5. d

A long time with no rain, called a drought, could cause a problem for the Incas. When there was a drought, not as much food could be grown. If there was not enough food, the ayllus, or families, could barely feed themselves. When there was no extra food, the leaders could not tax the people. Without the tax, the Incas could not afford to make more roads or bridges and they could not repair damaged roads either.

The Concert (descriptive) 48
Descriptions will vary. Paragraphs will vary, but should use the senses to describe.
1. taste
2. sound or sight
3. sound
4. sight
5. touch or sight
6. sight
7. smell
8. sight, sound, or smell

You Need a Pencil (how-to) 49
1. b
2. a

Penguins and Puffins (compare and contrast) 50
Possible answers listed. They can be in any order.
1. a. both sea birds
   b. both swim well
   c. black and white feathers
2. a. puffins can fly, penguins cannot
   b. puffins live in northern hemisphere, penguins live in southern hemisphere
   c. penguins lay one to two eggs, puffins lay one egg per season

Can I Keep It? (persuasive) 51
1. a
2. c
3. c

Paragraphs will vary, but should include the three reasons listed in answers 1–3.

Scuba Diving (multiple paragraphs) 52
a

To Test or Not To Test (five-paragraph essay) 53
Sentences to be underlined and written in paragraph form:
State tests try to find out if the educational system is working as it should.
First, it is vital to know that students are learning what is being taught.
Also, these tests may show whether the school is teaching the right skills in the right way.

Answer Key

Another reason to test is so each state can measure how well all of the schools are doing.
These tests may help your classes improve.
Concluding sentence: Used well, testing can be helpful.

Nine Lives (recognizing narratives) 54
1. E
2. N
3. N
4. E
5. N

Parts (beginning, middle, end) 55
1. end
2. beginning
3. middle
4. end
5. middle
6. beginning

In the Beginning (setting)..............................56
1. d, V
2. f, VI
3. c, II
4. a, III
5. e, I
6. b, IV

Fillmore Ice Boys (characterization) 57
1. tall, questioning eyes; not smartest or toughest but never gives up
2. a little chubby, dark eyes; kind and gentle, could look at you to your heart, tells stories about Alaska
3. short, long face, quick movements; shivers all the time, happy
4. very short hair, speaks fast; loud, always excited, thinks he's like Tom Sawyer

Let Me Introduce You (characterization) 58
1. a
2. c
3. Answers will vary, but should demonstrate a wise and fair king.

Conflicting Stories (conflict) 59
1. a
2. c
3. Answers will vary, but should include the fact that the girls are lost.

Cheeser and the Cat (plot/events) 60
1. a, f, g, i
2. a
3. Answers will vary.

In the End (resolution)................................61
1. a. plot; b. resolution; c. plot
2. Answers will vary.

When the Chips Are Down (story structure) 62-63
1. summer, before the science fair; Dexter's garage
2. Dexter, Sean, Mrs. Frommer, Dexter's mother
3. Dexter and Sean need a computer chip to make their science fair robot work correctly.
4. First, they try to repair the chip they have.
5. Next, Dex tries to borrow money from his mother to buy the chip they need.
6. Then, the boys try to earn money to buy a chip.
7. Mrs. Frommer gives them a coupon so they can afford the chip. At the fair, the boys' robot works.

What's the Point? (theme) 64
1. e
2. b
3. a
4. c
5. d

The New Kid (narrative planning) 65
1a. b, f
1b. d
1c. g
2. a
3. h
4. c
5. e

Whose Story Is It? (point of view) 66-67
1. omniscient
2. camera view
3. limited omniscient
4. first person
5. I held the bone so the dog could smell it. Then, I threw the bone far across the junkyard. The dog bolted after it. I hopped the fence and climbed onto the old shed. I looked for my mother's car.
6. Yolanda crossed her arms and leaned against the locker. She and Angel both scowled. Angel clenched her fist and kicked the wall over and over.
7. Answers will vary. Dede and Ona's feelings should both be reflected in the paragraph.

Lead the Reader (hooks) 68
1. b   2. a
3. b   4. c

Secret Agents (story transitions) 69
1. While Agent Jaquar climbed the outside wall
2. before the launch
3. Earlier that day
4. Meanwhile
5. While on patrol duty
6. a
7. d
8. c
9. b

Answer Key

◆◆

The Artist in Every Writer (show, don't tell) 70
1. tell
2. show
3. pictures will vary a great deal
4. should show a sun, grassy fields, and children flying kites
5. #4; It shows, it doesn't tell.
6. Answers will vary. All should "show" a hot day: people sweating, dogs panting, bright sun, etc.

Let Your Feelings Show (show, don't tell) 71
1. afraid
2. mad
3. very brave
Rewritten sentences will vary.
4. c   5. b
6. e   7. d
8. a

Mabel's Magic Cakes (show, don't tell) 72–73
1. Excitement rattled through the frozen crowd like a pin-ball.
2. He cradled the cake in his arms and carefully shuffled toward home.
3. "I saw colors—bright as jewels, flashing and racing in front of my eyes."
Answers 4, 5, and 6 will vary.
All answers on page 73 will vary.

The Nature of Nature (quotations) 74
1. "All nature wears one universal grin," stated Henry Fielding.
2. Ralph Waldo Emerson said, "Nature and books belong to the eyes that see them."
3. "Everything has its beauty," explains Confucius, "but not everyone sees it."
4. Albert Einstein said, "The most beautiful thing we can experience is the mysterious. It is the source of all true art and science."
5. As Aristotle said, "Nature does nothing uselessly."
6. "One touch of nature makes the whole world kin," stated William Shakespeare.

Who Said What? (indenting quotes) 75
1. a, c, d, f, h, i, m
2. "Look," said Jalie pointing to the ground.
   "What?" shouted Max.
   "Hush, Max. Let her talk," said Zee.
   "Well, there's not really a floor, but the walls are connected to boards," said Jalie.
   "So we could drag the fort somewhere else," said Craft. "Great thinking, Jalie!"

Gauthier's Gator (paragraphing/indentation) 76
Bekah walked along the raised, gravel road. She was anxious to reach her friend's house.
"Hi there, Mr. Gauthier," she called.
"Hello Bekah," he hollered back.
Bekah liked Mr. Gauthier. He was always working in his yard. Momma says that he grew the prettiest flowers in seven states. "I am sure that's true," said Bekah softly to herself.
As she rounded the corner, Bekah screamed. Peeking his snout out from under her friend Lana's house was the biggest alligator Bekah had ever seen! She froze. She knew not to get close to a gator.
Mr. Gauthier came running.

End of the Day (endings) 77
1. d
2. Answers will vary.

What's in a Name? (story titles) 78
1. c
2. Titles will vary, but should give a clue to the story without giving away the ending.
3. The Call of the Wild
4. A Wrinkle in Time
5. Bridge to Terabithia
6. Mrs. Frisby and the Rats of NIMH

The Sum of the Parts (narrative review) 79
Across
6. end
7. point of view
10. hook
11. climax
12. plot
13. beginning
14. characters

Down
1. transitions
2. middle
3. title
4. resolution
5. conflict
8. setting
9. dialogue

Whoosh! (onomatopoeia) 80
1. whooshed
2. snap
3. rattled
4. croak, chirping, bree-deep, caws, whistles, trills, buzz
5. Paragraphs will vary but should have at least six words that show onomatopoeia.

Jovial Jobs (consonance, alliteration, and assonance) 81
1. alliteration, f
2. consonance, d, b
3. assonance, long a
4. alliteration, r
5. assonance, long i
6. consonance, t
7. gathers them all together and tells them what there is to know

Answer Key

◆◆◆◆◆◆◆◆◆◆◆◆◆◆◆◆◆◆◆◆◆◆◆◆◆◆◆◆◆◆◆◆◆◆◆◆◆◆

8. travels from town to town, talking with farmers.
9. so he shows the whole set of tractors with photos.

Other examples are possible.

Smart as a Whip (similes) 82
1. swan
2. drums
3. fish
4. rock
5.–8. Similes will vary. All should be logically based on the hint sentences.

She is an Angel (metaphors) 83
1. c
2. b
3. c
4. c
5. b

6.–7. Metaphors will vary. All should follow logically from the given phrases.

Like a Dream (similes and metaphors) 84
1. M; he keeps everything.
2. S; she is kind and/or friendly.
3. S; he is out of control when angry.
4. M; he is untrustworthy; sneaky.
5. S; he was impossible to pin down or capture.
6. M; you are wonderful.
7. M; it has a range of many colors.
8. S; he is mean and/or on the attack.
9. S; I slept very well.
10. M; she reads constantly.

I Could Eat a Horse (hyperbole) 85
H: 1, 2, 4, 6, 7
Hyperboles 8-12 will vary. All should be extreme exaggerations.

Autumn is Alive (personification) 86
1. bullies, letting go, breathes, gets tired, goes to bed, dress in bright gowns, skipping, dancing, stretch their empty hands, drags a blanket, sleeps in, standing firm, hands on her hips, peers
2. invited to a costume party, wear, forget to change from their green clothes, wear the faded, brown suits they've worn too long, gather together, chatter, dance, arm in arm, swing, swirl, twist, twirl, dance, waltz, prattle on, arms, able to dance, plays a different song
Answers 3–8 will vary.

What Next? (foreshadowing) 87
1–3 all include foreshadowing. Ideas will vary.

The GTS Timebender (foreshadowing) 88
1. d
2. f
3. b
4. c

Science Fair (tone) 89
1. b   2. d
3. f   4. c
5. e   6. a
7. d   8. b

Get an Attitude! (tone) 90
Answers will vary. Ideas are listed below.
1. I brought my grade up from an "F" to a "C" on my math test today!
2. Even though I studied for three hours, I only got a "C" on my math test today.
3. Today, I scored 77% of the problems on my math test correctly and received a "C" grade.
4. a
5. a

A Toolbox (crossword review) 91
Across
2. hyperbole
7. metaphor
9. point of view
11. foreshadowing
12. alliteration

Down
1. consonance
3. assonance
4. onomatopoeia
5. simile
6. personification
8. hook
10. tone

The Northern Lights (prewriting—purpose/audience) 92
1. a, II
2. c, I
3. b, III
4. Persuasive paragraphs will vary, but should include supporting details from the paragraph supplied.

Aurora Borealis (prewriting—prompts) 93
1. expository
2. narrative
3. persuasive
4. persuasive
5. expository
6. narrative

Stories will vary.

A Most Unusual Light (revising—extraneous details) 94
Cross out in "Omens of the Northern Lights":
Tribes in the mountains and river valleys of South America never saw the northern lights. They had different omens based on the weather. A drought, a time with little water, meant that the gods were not happy.

Answer Key

◆◆◆◆◆◆◆◆◆◆◆◆◆◆◆◆◆◆◆◆◆◆◆◆◆◆◆◆◆◆◆◆◆

The Fox and Sauk tribes saw the northern lights, too.

Cross out in "Solar-Powered Light Show":
The wind on earth is made up of air molecules.
    Since the aurora is electrical, it can cause problems with radios and satellites.

More Details, Please (revising—elaboration) 95
1. a
2. b
3. b
Sentences 4 and 5 will vary, but should match the hints given.

Nature's Splendor (revising—specific writing) 96
1. c
2. a
3. b
4. c

Carlos's Wagon Wheel (revising—pronoun problems) 97
1. wagon wheel; Carlos
2. wheel
3. spare wheel or hammer; could be either one, although following sentence implies it's the spare wheel.
4. top of tree trunk
5. Carlos watched the wagon and the wagon wheel closely; he was afraid the wheel would break.
6. Carlos looked for a spare wheel and a hammer, but he could not find a spare wheel (or a hammer).

Too Slow and Steady (revising—sentences).....................98
Sentences may vary slightly.
1. The tortoise is slow and steady.
2. Tortoises are endangered because people harm their habitats.
3. Paragraphs will vary, but they should display varied sentences. "Have hinged shells." and "Use the shell to hide from predators" are the fragments.

Siva, from Bombay (editing—subjects and verbs) 99
1. Siva is from India, a country in Asia.
2. He came from a city called Bombay.
3. Next year, Siva will go to high school.
4. Corrected paragraph: Siva came to the United States to study. He left his family back in India. When he came to America, he told his family that he would miss them. Siva writes a letter to them every week. He tells them about his studies, his friends, and his life in the United States. Siva wants to be at teacher in India. After he studies for four years in America, he will go home to his family. He says he cannot wait to see them again. His family cannot wait, either. They miss him.

Corrections: left, came, (remove) Siva, them, will go, said or says, miss, him

Gum-Everlasting (editing—spelling) 100

Gum-Everlasting	Brother Be-Gone
Dose—Does	goed—went
gets—get	allways—always
too—to	Thay—they
Yule—You'll	laught—laughed
you're—your	tryed—tried
befor—before	Be-Gon—B-Gone
sotf—soft	Chessas—Chessa's
bye—buy	brotters—brothers
	could'nt—couldn't
	came—come
	hafe—have

Love, Grandpa (editing—punctuation/capitalization) 101
123 Memory Lane
El Monte, CA 92403
January 12, 2001
The hamburgers, potato salad, and homemade pie were all perfect.
Esther said, "That's the prettiest sweater I've ever seen!"
I am glad you love it, too. Let's get together to play and sing some more. Maybe I can even learn some of that electric guitar music that you play.

Break It Up (editing—paragraphing/indentation) 102
Indents: d, h, k, m, o, p, q, r, v, w, x

Short, But Sweet (short answers) 103
1. e
2. a

Get the Message (summarizing/theme) 104
1. c
2. c

Butterfly Girl (summarizing) 105
The correct summary is b.

Not My Words (paraphrasing) 106
1. b
2. a

Primary Colors (taking notes).....................................107
1. a
2. c
3. b

A Few Notes on Dogs (taking notes) 108
1. c
2. g or a
3. a or g
4. f
5. i or d
6. d or i

Answer Key

Giants of the Desert (outlining) 109
    I. A. 2.nine tons
    I. B. 2.can live 200 years
    II. B. only 10 inches of rainfall a year
    III. C. white, waxy flowers; Arizona State flower

Whose Fault Is It? (essay questions) 110
    1. b
    2. d
    3. a, c, d, e, g

It's Not My Fault (essay questions) 111
Answers will vary, but writing plan should include details from page 109 and sentence answers should include the key words from the questions.

Walking a Thin Line (summarizing) 112
    c

Neuschwanstein (summarizing) 113
    1. c

An Egyptian Thank-you (writing a letter) 114
    1. e. Hayes Elementary School (rest of address is correct)
    2. b. October 18, 2001
    3. f. Dear Mrs. Bradley,
    4. d. (no corrections)
    5. c. Very truly yours,
    6. a. (no corrections)

**Signed, Sealed, and Delivered
(addressing envelopes)** 115
    1. Nadine May Hayward
       298 Rose Lane
       Jackson, Mississippi 36946
    2. street number
    3. state
    4. Return addresses will vary, but should have all the components of a written address.
       Mrs. Helen Colles
       845 Pine Street
       Garnet, Montana 55608

Pebble Rings, Like Memories (poetry) 116
    1. like the songs that each of my memories sings
    2. Bay, play; Dad, had; rings, sings; Lenore, more; done, one, son
    3. seems like a kid
    4. like an older man, a father or grandfather
    5. sad—missing people in his family

Couplets and Quatrains (poetry—couplets) 117
    1. c
    2. e
    3. Answers will vary.
    4. Answers will vary, but should show a bb rhyme to fit into the aabb pattern in the quatrain.

Cleri-Who? (poetry—clerihews) 118
    1. b, f, g, d
    2. e, c, h, a
Additional clerihews will vary, but should follow the pattern.

Electric Etheree (poetry—etherees) 119
    a. 5
    b. 7
    c. 4
    d. 9
    e. 3
    f. 6
    1. And I have
    2. magnetic glow
    3. I shine like a light at night
    4. Am I a nightlight? Am I a boy?
    5. an electric shock
    6. The electricity drained from the bulb into the boy.